STEPHEN GOSSON

Princeton Studies in English
Volume 25

Stephen Gosson

A Biographical and Critical Study

BY WILLIAM RINGLER

OCTAGON BOOKS

A DIVISION OF FARRAR, STRAUS AND GIROUX

New York   1972

95658

Copyright, 1942, by Princeton University Press

Reprinted 1972
by special arrangement with Princeton University Press

OCTAGON BOOKS
A Division of Farrar, Straus & Giroux, Inc.
19 Union Square West
New York, N. Y. 10003

Library of Congress Cataloging in Publication Data

Ringler, William A., 1912-
    Stephen Gosson.
    Original ed. issued as vol. 25 of Princeton studies in
English series.
    A revision of the author's thesis, Princeton University, 1937.
        Bibliography: p.
        1. Gosson, Stephen, 1554-1624. I. Series: Princeton
        University. Princeton studies in English, v. 25.
[PR2279.G6Z7 1972]   828'.3'09 [B]   79-159222
ISBN 0-374-96814-4

Manufactured by Braun-Brumfield, Inc.
Ann Arbor, Michigan

Printed in the United States of America

PREFACE

This study was originally prepared, and in 1937 was
accepted by the Department of English of Princeton University,
in partial fulfillment of the requirements for the degree of
Doctor of Philosophy. It has since been completely revised
and a good deal of new material has been added.

Complete bibliographical information concerning works
cited in the text is contained in the footnotes, which are
numbered consecutively through each chapter. In the case of
works by Gosson, references to the Ephemerides and the Trumpet
of Warre are to the folios of the first editions; references
to the Schoole of Abuse and the Apologie are to the folios of
the first editions and to the pages of Arber's reprint; and
references to Playes Confuted are to the folios of the first
edition and to the pages of the reprint by W. C. Hazlitt in
The English Drama and Stage.

The collection of material for this work was made possible
only by the generous cooperation of many institutions of learning and individual scholars. I have acknowledged various
specific obligations at appropriate places in the text; but I
want to take the opportunity here to make a general statement
of my indebtedness. I wish to thank the authorities of the
Bodleian Library, the British Museum, the Dulwich College
Library, the H. E. Huntington Library, the Princeton University
Library, and the A. S. W. Rosenbach Company for permission to
read and quote books and manuscripts in their collections. I
am indebted to the members of the staffs of these institutions,
and especially to Professor M. W. Young, Reference Librarian
of the Princeton University Library, for many kindly acts of
assistance. Professor Mark Eccles, Professor J. G. Milne, Miss
M. N. M. O'Farrell, the Reverend T. A. Talbot-Thomas, and the
Reverend F. Yates have generously provided me with biographical
information concerning Gosson and with transcripts of records
in English archives. Mr. C. K. Edmonds, Professor J. S. Finch,
Captain R. B. Haselden, Professor V. B. Heltzel, Miss Eugenia
Osborne, Professor F. B. Williams, Jr., and W. S. Wright, Esq.,
have given me aid in the solution of bibliographical problems.
I am also indebted for various items of information to
Professor M. M. Knappen, Professor Kathrine Koller, Doctor
Stephen Whicher, and Doctor Curt A. Zimansky.

My greatest obligations, however, are to Professor H. H. Hudson, under whose direction this study was first undertaken, who guided my researches and provided me with much information from his great knowledge of things Elizabethan; to Professor G. H. Gerould, who read the final draft of the manuscript and offered many helpful suggestions; and to Dean R. K. Root, who has been an unfailing source of advice, kindly criticism, and encouragement.

William Ringler

Miami Beach
October 3, 1942

TABLE OF CONTENTS

CHAPTER I: THE STUDENT

i

Stephen Gosson, who was in turn a playwright, a pamphleteer, and a clergyman, has a small but certain place in all histories of Elizabethan literature. His chief claim to attention
is his publication, in 1579, of the Schoole of Abuse, the most
important of the tracts in the Elizabethan anti-stage controversy and itself a prime cause of that lively pamphlet war of
the late seventies and early eighties. He also deserves mention for his part in introducing and popularizing the "new
English" that contemporaries called Euphuism, and must be
given credit for being a successful and, in his own time,
highly popular author of the kind of literature that was the
Elizabethan counterpart of the novel.

He was a talented, although not a great, writer, and his
vigorous and witty essays are still interesting and entertain-
ing; though the historical importance of his works is even
greater than their artistic excellence. The commercial development of England had brought the new middle class into prominence. With the spread of education, the members of this
group became an important part of the reading public, so that
the writers of the time found it profitable to appeal to their
tastes and necessary to respect their prejudices. Suspicious
of innovation, insistent upon morality, and utilitarian in
their views, the members of the middle class demanded that
literature and the drama should not be frivolous, and should
serve some worthy purpose. It is because Gosson expressed so
perfectly the ideas of this practical, serious, and moral
middle class, of which he was himself a member and to which
he addressed his pamphlets, that his works are of special
significance to the historian of Elizabethan life and letters.

Through no merit of his own, but by a fortunate accident
of circumstance, Gosson's life and writings are also of interest because they exemplify the influence Elizabethan educational institutions exerted upon the mode of thought and manner of expression of their pupils. It has been possible to
recover considerable information about the course of his studies while he was in residence at Oxford; even some of the academic lectures he heard there have been preserved. As he was
a careful note-taker, and as ideas and illustrations from the

college lectures reappear frequently in his pamphlets, his
works furnish an example, unique so far as I am aware, of the
way in which the students of his time put to use the knowledge
they gained in the universities.

Sir Sidney Lee collected all that was known about the life
of Gosson in his article in the Dictionary of National Biography. I have been able to supplement his bare outline with many
new documents and a good deal of collateral material, so the
following pages contain at least something more than a name and
a collection of dates. Unfortunately, there was no Fuller to
strike out a series of deft phrases on Gosson's character, no
Aubrey to leave a few "brief lies" with which to spice the narrative of his doings, no collection of private correspondence
to show him in informal attire as well as in full dress. Lacking, as we do, these short cuts to characterization, I have
tried to provide a substitute by discussing in some detail the
men with whom he came in contact and the ideas by which he was
influenced. I hope that doing this will shed some light, if
not directly upon his personality, at least indirectly upon
the complex and interesting age in which he lived.

Stephen, the eldest son and second child of Cornelius
Gosson, was baptized in the church of St. George the Martyr,
Canterbury, April 17, 1554.[1] We know very little of his an-

---

1. The Register Booke of the Parish of St. George the
Martyr, ed. J.M. Cowper (Privately Printed, 1891), contains the
following entries relating to Stephen Gosson and his family:

Christenings

14 Aug. 1551.   Agnes Goosen, d. of Cornelys Goosen.
17 Apr. 1554.   Stephan, s. of Cornelys Gooson.
28 Mar. 1558.   Will'm, s. of Cornelius Gosson.
11 Feb. 1560/1. Johne Gossyn and Joane Gossyn, the daughters
                [sic] of Cornelius Gossyn.
 8 Feb. 1563/4. Dorothie, d. of Cornelys Gossen.

Marriages

18 Jul. 1546.   Cornelius Gostson and Agnes Oxenbridge.
15 Jul. 1577.   Thomas Barker and Agnes Gosson.

Burials

12 Feb. 1560/1. Joan, d. of Cornelys Gossyn.
 2 Jul. 1562.   John, s. of Cornelys Gossan.
31 Oct. 1574.   Agnes, wyfe of Cornelius Gosson.
 3 Aug. 1577.   An [sic], wife of Thomas Barker.

J. M. Cowper first called attention to the record of
Stephen's baptism in N&Q, 8th ser., III (1893), 346. I have
found no record of the burial of his father, Cornelius. By
1622 his youngest sister, Dorothy, was married and had a

cestors and relatives outside of his own immediate family. The
Gossons in the sixteenth century were a numerous band, living
for the most part in the southern counties of England, and it
is impossible to say in what way the various persons bearing
that surname were related, if all.[2] None of them were titled,
though some were substantial, even wealthy, citizens. There
was a Richard, London goldsmith, deputy of his ward, member of
the Company of East India merchants, and friend of Edward
Alleyn the actor; a Thomas, member of the Stationers' Company
and one of the lesser Elizabethan booksellers; and a Gerard,
physician, compiler of an almanac for the year 1571, and active
theological controversialist.[3] But most of the name were small
farmers, petty tradesmen, or persons even lower in the social
and economic scale.

---

daughter, for in his will he left fifty pounds to "my welbeloved sister Dorothye Mansworth (the wiffe of William Mansworth)
of newe Castle," and another fifty pounds to "my welbeloved
neece Dorothye Mansworth." Apparently Dorothy died before 1629,
as she is not mentioned in William's will, though her daughter,
now "Dorothy Goodwin widdow dwellinge at New Castle," received
a considerable legacy. For further details concerning William,
see Appendix A.
     2. The vagaries of Elizabethan spelling make identifica-
tion of the name difficult. Stephen's father was variously
referred to in official records as Gostson, Goosen, Gosson,
etc., though Stephen invariably signed himself Gosson. If we
are to believe Barnabe Rich, who referred to Stephen in a sonnet prefacing Lodge's An Alarum against Usurers, in the line
"Thou needst not feare Goose sonne or Ganders hisse," the name
was pronounced with a long o; but Rich was probably using pho-
netic as well as poetic license for the purpose of satire.
Whatever its pronunciation, the name was fairly common. I
have come upon sixteenth-century records of almost a hundred
separate individuals who had Gosson, in some one of its various spellings, for a surname, and I have not included Goschen
as a legitimate variant. Stephen's ancestors may have been
Flemings or French--there were Gossons in the Low Countries
and France; but the name, which is found in Kent as early as
1300, is also of English origin, being a derivative of either
the characteristic surname Goodson or the local surname Gosden.
     3. Sir Sidney Lee says in the D.N.B. that Thomas (who
was the publisher of Playes Confuted) was probably Stephen's
brother; the suggestion is highly improbable, though they may
have been more distantly related. For Gerard, see my article
in N&Q, CLXXIX (1940), 203-4, and A. W. Haggis, ibid., 282.

Stephen's parents were among the less distinguished of
this relatively undistinguished group. His mother, Agnes Oxenbridge, was probably daughter of a family whose sons had been
butchers and grocers in Canterbury for a century.[4] His father,
a joiner by trade and a freeman of Canterbury, may have been a
descendant of the shoemaker, Gerard Gotson, who from 1461 to
1476 paid a yearly fee for the privilege of trading in the same
city.[5] Cornelius was evidently a poor man, for his eldest son
first became a scholar of the King's School, which supposedly
admitted only boys who were poor and destitute of friends, and
later a discipulus of Corpus Christi College, Oxford--discipuli
being students who had incomes of less than forty shillings a

---

4. The Canterbury parish registers were not begun early
enough to record Agnes's birth. Other records indicate that
there were at least three Oxenbridge families in the city early in the sixteenth century. The most likely hypothesis is
that she was the daughter of Thomas Oxenbridge (or Oxynbregge),
grocer, who became a freeman by redemption in 1519--see The
Roll of the Freemen of the City of Canterbury, ed. J. M. Cowper
(Canterbury, 1903), p. 290 and Archaeologica Cantiana, XXXIII
(1918), 40. Stephen's sermon, The Trumpet of Warre, was published by John Oxenbridge, the London stationer, and in his
will he left fifty shillings to "my Cozen Margaret Oxenbridge,"
who reappears in William's will as "my Cousin Margaret Chamflower."

5. The Roll of the Freemen, ed. Cowper, p. 101, records
that in 1577 Thomas Baroker, shoemaker, was made a freeman by
reason of his marriage to Agnes, daughter of Cornelius Gosson,
joiner. A man could become a freeman by marriage only if his
wife was the daughter of a freeman. Gerard is mentioned in
Intrantes: A List of Persons Admitted to Live and Trade Within the City of Canterbury, ed. J. M. Cowper (Canterbury, 1909),
pp. 107-26. The next record of the surname in Canterbury is
the marriage of Cornelius in 1546. There were also several
Gossons who were small farmers in nearby Thanet. The attack
on Stephen entitled Straunge Newes out of Affrick contained "a
dirtie comparison of a dutch Mule and an english mare, that
ingendred an Asse" (Ephemerides, fol. A2), which indicates
that the anonymous author thought that Cornelius, or at least
his ancestors, came from the Low Countries. Gerard Gotson, if
indeed he was the founder of the English branch of the family,
was very probably a Fleming, for Cowper, in the forward to his
edition of Intrantes, says that in the early and middle years
of the fifteenth century many Flemish shoemakers emigrated to
Canterbury.

year.[6] Furthermore, the fact that there is no record of his
will or of a grant of administration for his estate probably
indicates that he had no property worth disposing of.

Stephen's family, therefore, was one of humble circumstances and belonged, socially, to the lower middle class.
Years later he had to endure in silence the taunts of his enemy Lodge on his "base degree."[7] But, as the old rime said,

When Adam delved and Eve span
Who was then the gentleman?

In Elizabethan days the feudal aristocracy was breaking up, and
it was possible for a man of no ancestry to acquire a coat of
arms, or even be made a peer of the realm, if he distinguished
himself sufficiently. Lord Burghley could not trace his family
back more than two generations, and even the Queen's own great-
grandfather had been a London merchant.

Like many other members of the middle class, Cornelius
Gosson was apparently ambitious for the material, social, and
intellectual advancement of his family. He could not provide
his son with much in the way of worldly goods, but he did make
an effort to give him a good education. Thus in 1568 we find
Stephen a King's scholar of the cathedral school at Canterbury.[8] As a scholar he received free tuition and a stipend
of about four pounds a year to pay for his commons and cloth-
ing. The entrance requirements he had to meet were that he
be able to read and write and be moderately versed in the
rudiments of Latin grammar. He could hardly have learned
sufficient Latin at home to qualify for admission; but there
was an elementary school supported by the city corporation
which he may have attended, or he may have become a cathedral chorister, learned his A.B.C.'s at the choir school, and
graduated to the grammar school after his voice had changed
and he was no longer of any use as a singer. His comparatively advanced age (he was fourteen) when he was appointed
as a King's scholar seems to bear out this last supposition.

At the King's School the boys were supposed to attend
"until they have obtained a moderate acquaintance with the
Latin grammar, and have learned to speak in Latin and write

---

6. C. E. Woodruff and H. J. Cape, Schola Regia
Cantuariensis (1908), p. 346, and Thomas Fowler, The History of
Corpus Christi College (Oxford, 1893), p. 46. Information in
the following pages about the King's School and Corpus is from
these works.

7. An Alarum against Usurers (1584), fol. A4; see also
his Reply to Gosson (1579), fol. C6[v].

8. Woodruff and Cape, Schol. Reg. Cant., p. 90.

in Latin; for which object they shall be allowed the space of
four years." Stephen apparently spent the stipulated time in
the usual exercises of memorizing, translating, varying sentences, writing short compositions, and studying the works of
Cicero, Virgil, Ovid, Terence, Sallust, and the other authors
contained in the usual curriculum of an Elizabethan grammar
school. Instruction in Greek was also given, though this probably did not extend beyond a few select readings in the New
Testament. That his training was thorough is shown by the
frequency with which he quoted the grammar school authors in
his later published writings.

Another important part of the boys' activities, as at
other schools, was the acting of plays. References in the
treasurer's accounts show that the students performed English
plays, possibly of their own composition, as well as the
traditional Latin plays. Also, companies of professional
actors frequently came to Canterbury on summer tour. Between
1554 and 1572 no fewer than seventeen groups of players made
a total of forty visits to the cathedral city, and of these
Leicester's men returned at least six times. So Stephen had
ample opportunity--either as spectator, actor, or playwright,
perhaps all three--to gain the dramatic experience he later
turned to account when he set his "cunning abroache, by pen-
ning Tragedies, and Comedies in the Citte of London."[9] He
was not the only Canterbury boy to be attracted by the stage.
His contemporary John Lyly made a name for himself as a writer of brilliant court comedies, and Christopher Marlowe, ten
years his junior, gained an even greater reputation in the
field of tragedy.

But the ideal of sixteenth-century pedagogy was the pius
literatus, the man liberally educated in moral disciplines;
and if school plays and London actors drew the minds of the
boys to the glamour of the theater and the delights of the
city, the masters just as certainly tried to impress them
with the joys of right living and the rewards of godliness.
Fully as important as the study of Latin and Greek in the
King's School was the instruction given in sound principles
of religion and morality, conformable to the two-fold provision of the statutes that the masters should "train up in
piety and adorn with sound learning" the pupils given into
their charge. As the school was an appendage of the Cathedral, the injunction to train up in piety was obeyed even
more strictly than in the other grammar schools of the kingdom, especially as Archbishop Parker himself selected the

---

9. Playes Confuted, fol. B, p. 167.

masters and suggested methods of instruction. Gosson acquitted himself well as a student for, in the report of a visitation of the school made by the Archbishop in 1570, his name
was placed fourth on the list of fifty grammarians.[10] He
apparently completed the four-year course with a desire for
further education, because the next notice of him at the end
of that period is as a student at Oxford.

ii

Gosson's name was entered in the admission book of Corpus
Christi College, Oxford, April 4, 1572.[11] His years at the
University were the most important of his life, for during his
stay there his character was moulded to a pattern from which
it never seems to have deviated, while the knowledge he acquired furnished most of the material contained in his published writings. An account of the men with whom he came in
contact and of the course of his studies will explain many
aspects of his later career.

According to Izaak Walton, at the time of Gosson's
residence Corpus was "noted for an eminent library, strict
students, and remarkable scholars." This was no idle pane-
gyric. The college had been founded in 1516 by Richard Foxe,
Bishop of Winchester, to be a "bee-hive" of learning, and had
numbered among its early fellows and lecturers Vives, Lupset,
Pole, and Jewel. Its fame as a house of learning had suffered no diminution in the fifty-odd years since its foundation, and Gosson had as associates a group of men who later
became eminently distinguished for their scholarship and for
their activities in the affairs of Church and State. Eight
of them, including Gosson himself, have their names enshrined
in that retrospective Who's Who, the Dictionary of National
Biography.

The most famous of the company was Richard Hooker, who

---

10. Registrum Matthei Parker, ed. W. H. Frere (Oxford,
1907-33), II, 535.

11. Fowler, Hist. Corpus, p. 390. Aside from this entry,
and the entries of his supplication for and admission to the
B.A. degree, there is no other record of Gosson's residence at
Oxford. Dr. J. G. Milne, the librarian of Corpus, kindly informed me that there is "no record concerning him in the College archives, beyond the usual admission entries." Gosson
was admitted as a discipulus, which means that he was given a
room in the college, free commons, and a small annual stipend
for incidental expenses.

had entered about five years before Gosson and was laying the
foundation for that monument of Elizabethan philosophy and
theology, the Laws of Ecclesiastical Polity. He had in his
charge two boys, Edwin Sandys and George Cranmer, who later
rose to important positions of state. Next to Hooker in
eminence was John Rainolds, who during the period of Gosson's
residence was Greek reader of the college. Rainolds was a
vigorous controversialist and was still famous, even in
Walton's time, "for the learned and wise menage of a public
dispute with John Hart (of the Romish persuasion) about the
head and faith of the church." He afterwards became dean of
Lincoln, and later president of Corpus, though his most important work was done as foreman of the Hampton Court conference,
at which he was instrumental in bringing about the translation
that is now known as the Authorized Version of the Bible. His
name is most familiar to literary students, however, for the
part he took, in 1592, in a controversy with William Gager in
which he opposed the lawfulness of acting plays. After
Rainolds's death John Spenser, another of Gosson's fellow
students, succeeded him as president of Corpus. He became
a noted preacher, was also engaged on the new version of the
Bible, was appointed chaplain to James I, and edited the
works of Hooker.

    That Corpus should have turned out so many prominent
theologians was only to be expected, for theology, in the words
of the founder, was "the science which we have always so highly
esteemed, that this our bee-hive has been constructed solely
or mainly for its sake." It was compulsory for the fellows of
the college to take orders. With the exception of Cranmer and
Sandys, all of Gosson's associates whose subsequent careers
can be traced served the Church in one capacity or another;
and even Sandys wrote an anti-Catholic polemic entitled
Speculum Europae. In addition to those who have already been
mentioned, John Barefoot became archdeacon of Lincoln and a
vigorous opponent of Puritanism, Samuel Beck canon of Exeter,
Henry Parry successively bishop of Gloucester and Worcester
and chaplain to Queen Elizabeth, while others held various
benefices or distinguished themselves as preachers. With such
early associates, it is not surprising that Gosson, only a few
years after he left the University, should have become a clergyman.

    Gosson, merely because he attacked the stage, has been
labelled a Puritan; but anyone who takes the trouble to read
his later writings or to investigate the circumstances of his
early life, finds that the description is without foundation.
The theology of the members of Corpus was the moderate Calvin-
ism prevalent in the Church of England at that time. Corpus,

in fact, was the home of Anglican apologetics. John Jewel, whose Apologia pro Ecclesia Anglicana (1562) was the first methodical statement of the position of the Church of England, had been lecturer on rhetoric there before the reign of Mary. Frequent references in correspondence and other documents of the 1570's show how greatly the members of his college respected his opinions, and in later years Gosson himself paid him eloquent tribute.[12] Up to the time of his death in 1571, Jewel had been the patron of Richard Hooker, who was the great moderator among all parties and at the same time one of the ablest champions of Episcopacy against Presbyterianism. When he delivered the morning sermons at the Temple in 1585, Hooker found himself opposed to Walter Travers, a noted Puritan, who gave the afternoon sermons. As Thomas Fuller expressed it, "The pulpit spake pure Canterbury in the morning, and Geneva in the afternoon, until Travers was silenced."

Hooker's tutor at Corpus, and his life-long friend, was John Rainolds. Though Rainolds was not so moderate as Hooker, and though he leaned more toward Geneva than Canterbury, he was not a strict Puritan. His early published works, Sex Theses (1580) and the Summe of the Conference (1584), reveal him as an earnest disciple of Jewel and a staunch defender of the Establishment. From his later years there is on record a letter he wrote to Bishop Bancroft in which he professed himself "huic Anglicanae ecclesiae conformem esse libenter et ex animo."[13] Indeed, it could almost be said that Hooker and Rainolds collaborated, Rainolds confuting the enemies of the Church of England in his De Romanae Ecclesiae Idolatria, and Hooker defending the principles upon which it was established in his Laws of Ecclesiastical Polity.

As the study of his writings later in this volume will show, Gosson was an imitator, not an initiator, and took most

---

12.   See his Trumpet of Warre, fols. E6^V, G.
13.   Quoted by Bliss in his edition of a Wood's Athenae Oxonienses, II, 14; see also Fowler, Hist. Corpus, p. 166. Most of the statements concerning Rainolds's Puritanism come from Anthony a Wood, who had a Puritan phobia and on such matters is not to be trusted. Crakanthorpe, in the Defensio Ecclesiae Anglicanae, published an elaborate defence of Rainolds's orthodoxy and showed, by references to his published works, that he approved of Episcopal government and the ceremonies of the Anglican Church. That his orthodoxy had been called in question was the result of the acrimony of controversy, for Rainolds was the most active and skilful opponent of Roman Catholicism in his generation.

of his opinions from his early associates at school and college.
It therefore seems extremely unlikely that, educated as he was
at the cathedral school in Canterbury, the seat of the Archbishop, and at Oxford surrounded by men who at that time were
no friends to Cartwright and no enemies to the Establishment,
he should have become in any strict sense of the term a Puritan.
The probability becomes a certainty when we find him, later in
life, violently attacking Presbyterianism and staunchly support-
ing the Puritan-hater, Bishop Bancroft. Instead of being a
Puritan, he actually was an active opponent of Puritanism,
which is no more than we should expect from a person under the
influence of the Anglican traditions of Corpus. On the other
hand, it is equally true that Gosson was educated in traditions
of strict morality and that he came in contact with men who
considered certain pleasures, which we today would call harm-
less amusements, to be the Devil's baits. But morality is not
the monopoly of any particular sect, and the serious Anglicans
of his time were as precise and unfavorable in their judgment
of worldly amusements as were the most rabid Puritans.

iii

As an undergraduate working for his B.A. degree, Gosson
was given a thorough training in logic and rhetoric and, after
he had completed eight or ten terms, he was required to take
part in the disputations held in the university schools in
order to put into practice the precepts he had learned. The
nature, and even the subjects, of these exercises are well
exemplified in the three essays, or rather orations, which
compose his second published work, the Ephemerides of Phialo.
Indeed, his treatises on the method of rebuking a friend, on
the ideal prince, and on right moral philosophy are so similar
in both content and structure to the academic disputations of
his time that they may very well have been elaborations on
themes given him to discuss as an undergraduate.

Of Gosson's teachers we know the names of three: Roger
Charnock, who was Latin reader; Richard Hooker, who gave
instruction in logic; and John Rainolds, who was Greek
reader. Of these Rainolds, who was an exceptionally effective
teacher, had by far the greatest influence with the students.
One of his pupils, Richard Crakanthorpe, later said of him:

> When we were young students...Dr. Reinolds
> conversed with us so familiarly and so profitably,
> that whatsoever, how often soever, how much so-
> ever any man desired to learn from him in any
> kind of knowledge, we daily drew it from his mouth,
> as an ever-springing and never-failing well. For

he had turned over (as I conceive) all writers, profane, ecclesiastical, and Divine...he was most excellent in all tongues...of a sharp and nimble wit,
of a grave and mature judgment, of indefatigable industry...so well seen in all arts and sciences as if
he had spent his whole time in each of them...In a
word, so modest, courteous, affable, and sweet was
his carriage, that though he were to be ranked above
the highest, yet he made himself equal in a manner
with the lowest.[14]

The book upon which Rainolds lectured was Aristotle's
Rhetoric, and the copy from which he read (Paris, 1562) is now
in the Bodleian Library, interleaved and containing copious
manuscript notes. But of even greater interest is a collection of twelve of the lectures themselves, which were published after his death by his friend and pupil Henry Jackson, and
another collection, in manuscript and still unpublished, in
the library of Queen's College.[15] An account of these lectures
is appropriate here, not only because of their independent
value in exemplifying concretely the kind of instruction that
was given to university undergraduates in the sixteenth century,
but also because Gosson himself apparently took careful notes
while he listened to them, and later embodied many of Rainolds's
ideas, and even modes of expression, in his own writings.
   The most striking thing about Rainolds's lectures is their
style. It is true that he advised his pupils to use rhetorical
figures with decency and moderation, told them not to overload
their compositions with too much ornament, and urged them to
have more care for things than for words, for truth than for
display. But his own practice was singularly at variance with
this portion of his teaching; or if not, then his conception

---

14. Defensio Ecclesiae Anglicanae (1625), cap. lxix;
translated by Daniel Featley in "The Life and Death of John
Reinolds," printed in Thomas Fuller's Abel Redevivus, ed. Wm.
Nichols (1867), II, 227.
   15. For information about the manuscripts and editions
of Rainolds's lectures, see the introduction and notes to his
Oratio in Laudem Artis Poeticae, ed. and tr. by William Ringler and Walter Allen, Jr. (Princeton, 1940), pp. 3-4, 7, 80.
References in the following pages are to the Huntington Library copy of the second edition of Jackson's collection, D.
Ioannis Rainoldi, Olim Graecae Linguae Praelectoris in Colle-
gio Corporis Christi apud Oxonienses, Orationes Duodecim; cum
aliis quibusdam opusculis (1619).

of moderation was somewhat peculiar. The very lecture in which
he warned his students against the excessive use of agnomina-
tiones, similiter cadentia and similiter desinentia (pp. 330-
31) jingled on every page with alliteration and rime. Another
rhetorical device of which he was particularly fond was the
accumulation of illustrative examples, which he recommended by
saying: "Multis exemplis...et historiis, carminibus, apophthegmatis, allusionibus venustissime quasi gemmis, disputationem
distingueret" (p. 432). It does not need a second glance at
his prose to see that it is the Latin counterpart of Euphuism.
Gosson, along with Lyly, Lodge, and others who were students at
Oxford during the time that he was delivering his lectures,
copied the style from him and introduced it into English.

The sixteenth century accepted Quintilian's definition of
an orator, as vir bonus dicendi peritus, and emphasized the
bonus (p. 3). It is therefore not surprising to find that
some of Rainolds's lectures, ostensibly based on Aristotle's
Rhetoric, are short treatises on Christian ethics. Most of
his orations show a decidedly theological and moralistic bias,
and like St. Augustine, he believed that the justification of
profane learning lay in the assistance it gives to divine stu-
ies. "Studeamus profanis artibus," he said, "sed referantur
ad Sacras" (p. 181). In this, as he remarked, he was following
the ideal of the founder of his college: "Haec sine controver-
sia, fuit voluntas illius pii Senis Richardi Foxi...ut religio,
ut pietas, ut sacra studia propagarentur" (p. 181). But scholarship and preaching are only means, not ends in themselves.
The contemplative must be combined with the active life, and
all studies must have as their object virtuous deeds; so
Rainolds insisted that his students should be actores as well
as oratores (p. 289). He devoted a whole lecture to elaborating this theme, and Gosson faithfully summarized his arguments in the Schoole of Abuse (fols. E-E3^V, pp. 50-2).

Rainolds was more a product of the Reformation than of
the Renaissance, so that his interests were specifically
religious rather than broadly humanistic. In fact, he was
definitely opposed to the liberal humanistic ideal of the
well-rounded man whose whole being, both mental and physical,
was harmoniously developed. Pay no attention to the body, he
said, take care only of the soul. Heed what "a Catone memo-
ratum est olim, et viris prudentibus meditandum est semper, id
vobis e memoria nunquam elabatur; Magna cura corporis, magna
est animi incuria" (p. 318). Gosson obeyed the injunction,
wrote the phrase down in his notebook, and in Playes Confuted
repeated Rainolds's argument, in part translating literally
his very words: we should not indulge ourselves in merely
physical pleasures, he said, for to do so "was longe agoe con-

demned by the heathen Cato, whose opinion is registred to be this, that such carefulness of our bodies, is a carelesnes of our vertues" (fol. E7^V, p. 199).

These being Rainolds's aims and ideals, it is not surprising to find him hostile to polite literature. It is true that in his later years he exclaimed, "You had like reason to aske whether wee did despise learned poetrie, which you were sure we did not,"[16] and that in his youth he had composed an Oratio in Laudem Artis Poeticae; but in his lectures he pointed out that in poetry there is always some bad mixed with whatever good it may contain (p. 308); and remarked that, like St. Augustine, he wished that no one were allowed to read secular poets, for "sermo profanus, animus Christianus non conveniunt" (p. 158).[17] The defense and attack are really not inconsistent. Poetry as an art is neither good nor bad in itself, it is the uses to which it is put that come up for criticism. As Gosson was later to explain, some "thinke that I banishe Poetrie, wherein they dreame...He that readeth with advise the booke which I wrote, shal perceive that I touche but the abuses of all these" (Apologie, fol. L2^V, p. 65). At the same time, with Rainolds, he was suspicious of an instrument that had such potentialities for evil as well as for good: "I must confesse that Poets are the whetstones of wit, notwithstanding that wit is dearly bought: where hony and gall are mixed, it will be hard to sever the one from the other" (Schoole of Abuse, fol. A2, p. 20).

Rainolds not only feared the effect of pagan poets upon English morals, he also feared the effect of pagan philosophy upon the Christian religion. "O quantum inter nos et Ethnicos interest!" he exclaimed (p. 158). The authority of Scripture, not the authority of Aristotle, was for him supreme. "Nam si nos ab Aristotele leviter declinemus, ut veritatem tueamur, quas commovent tragoedias?" (p. 439). He made no attempt, as the schoolmen of the Middle Ages and the scholars of the Renaissance had done, to harmonize Greek philosophy with Christian theology, and even went so far as to say that "quibus in locis Aristoteles regnat, illic impietas maxime dominatur" (p. 181). He attacked the Socratic nihil scio with such telling arguments (p. 466) that Gosson repeated them all in his Ephemerides (fols. A8^V-B2^V). He devoted a whole series of lectures to destructive

---

16. Th' Overthrow of Stage-Playes (n.p., 1599), p. 59.
17. Gosson likewise abjured profane studies for reasons similar to those given by Rainolds (Playes Confuted, fol. A2-2^V, p. 162). See also John Lyly, Works, ed. R. W. Bond (Oxford, 1902), I, 287.

criticism of Aristotle's notion of the Summum Bonum, which had
to be false because Aristotle was a pagan, for only "vera religio est vera beatitudo" (p. 185). In his judgment, Aristotle'
Felix and the Arabian Phoenix were cousin germans, neither
existed (p. 213). The statement provided both Gosson and Lyly
with a simile.[18]

Rainolds also attacked the traditional Aristotelian logic
and criticized the dialectical subtleties of the disputations
in the university schools, where the students "contortulas
tanta siccitate torquent conclusiunculas" (p. 436). In this,
as in most other things, Gosson followed him and devoted a
section of his Schoole of Abuse (fol. E2-2^V, p. 51) to a criticism of "those lither contemplators" of Oxford "which sit
concluding of Sillogismes in a corner."

But in tearing down one authority Rainolds set up another,
and instead of Aristotle he made Holy Scripture the final court
of appeal in all cases of controversy. Let all studies be compared to Scripture as a norm, he said (p. 310); let the fathers
of the early church be our guides and the Bible the arbiter of
all disputes (p. 127). This legalistic habit of mind, which
was not peculiar to Rainolds, accounts for the nature of much
of the controversial writing of the sixteenth century. The
Bible was the supreme court from which no appeal was allowed,
not even a referendum to common sense and natural reason. To
cite chapter and verse from Scripture in support of a point was
to carry it absolutely and without opposition. The workings of
this method of argumentation are nowhere better exemplified
than in Gosson's sermon The Trumpet of Warre, in which he ad-
vocated continuation of the war with Spain, not so much by reference to contemporary events or the political situation, as by
the accumulation of a series of Biblical texts.

Though Gosson profited in many ways from Rainolds's teaching, it is evident that, during his residence as a student in
Oxford at least, he did not hear arguments against the stage
from him. If he did, he probably never would have become a
playwright. Aside from a single short quotation from Seneca
on the folly of wasting time at theaters (p. 74), which was
introduced for quite another purpose, there is no indication
of opposition to the drama in Rainolds's lectures. In his
youth he had even acted in an academic play, had taken a
woman's part, that of Hippolyta, in Richard Edwardes's Pala-
mon and Arcyte at Christ Church in 1566. There is nothing
extraordinary about his tolerance at this period, because
prior to the building of the theaters outside London in 1576

---

18. Ephemerides, fol. D2; Lyly, Works, I, 260.

there was little or no spirit of antagonism to the stage evident in England. But a few years later his attitude changed, and in 1580, in the preface to his Sex Theses de Sacra Scriptura, et Ecclesia, he inveighed against the "pestes scenicorum, Theatralia spectacula" (p. 30), and in 1592, when he engaged in controversy with William Gager, he expressed violent disapproval even of the academic drama. But the arguments he later used in Th' Overthrow of Stage-Playes are so similar to those put forth in Playes Confuted, as at least to suggest the possibility that Gosson later consulted his former teacher when he entered upon his pamphleteering career.

Crakanthorpe's tribute to Rainolds's success as a teacher is given material illustration by the case of Gosson, for it is evident that from Rainolds he learned most of what he knew. He certainly copied his Euphuistic style from his Latin orations; his ideas about metaphysics, about dialectic, about moral philosophy, about theology, and about literature were in large part the product of his teaching; and his works abound with illustrations, echoes, and even direct quotations taken from his lectures. As Gosson was so profoundly influenced by his university training, it is likely that other men of letters of the time were similarly influenced. I think most of us have too uncritically accepted the grumblings of a few malcontents who complained that it was a waste of time to attend the universities, and from their statements have assumed that the seats of learning in the sixteenth century were suffering from intellectual stagnation. When more university lectures like those of Rainolds are made available for study, it will be seen that Oxford and Cambridge took a leading part in the vital intellectual concerns of Elizabethan England.

The kind of instruction Gosson received at Oxford, and the kind of persons with whom he came in contact, should effectually dispel the myth, for which he is himself partly responsible, that a sudden realization of the follies of his youth and a conversion to a stricter view of life made him attack the theater with which he had been so recently associated. Nothing could have been more serious or more strict than the view of life or the kind of morality that was impressed upon him at Canterbury and Oxford. Corpus was no friend to the Muses. Young men at that time who had a taste for literature went to Christ Church or some other of the Oxford colleges that looked with more favor upon the frivolous pastimes of poetizing and romancing. With the exception of Gosson himself, not one member of his college who was in residence during the years 1572-1576 was the author of a single published poem, play, or work of fiction. On the other hand, his associates did publish, during the course of their careers, some fifty volumes of sermons, religious tracts, and works of theological controversy.[19] Gosson's education thus made him, from the very beginning, a potential opponent of poetry and the drama, and his having slipped into the title of a playwright seems to have been the result of unfavorable circumstances and the necessity of earning his living, rather than of any deliberate choice of his own.

The exercises, what we should today call the examinations, for the B.A. degree at Oxford ordinarily began in or after a scholar's ninth term, when he appeared in the university schools and disputed with his fellow students in three questions on grammatical and logical subjects. As Gosson entered at the beginning of Easter term, 1572, in the normal course of events he would have engaged in these disputations in the Easter term of 1574. After that he was required to respond twice to the determining bachelors during Lent, which he probably did in the spring of 1575 and of 1576. Then, provided he completed the statutory residence requirement, he was at liberty to supplicate for his degree.[20]

Gosson apparently performed these exercises in the usual manner; and accordingly, in the autumn of 1576, he appeared before the required four successive congregations and asked leave to graduate. In due course, on October 31, his supplication was granted. Then, after he had been certified as "aptus et idoneus moribus et scientia," he was admitted to the degree of Bachelor of Arts, December 17, 1576,[21] "modo determinet proxima quadragesima"--provided he determine the following Lent. That is, although he had satisfied all the scholastic requirements, he had still to appear at St. Mary's in the

---

19. See the Short Title Catalogue under the names of Richard Hooker, Henry Hooke, Henry Parry, John Rainolds, Edwin Sandys, John Seller, William Smyth, John Spenser, and Richard Turnbull. The only work of a non-religious nature published by any of Gosson's fellows was a treatise on the celestial globe by Charles Turnbull.

20. For the exercises and formalities connected with taking the B.A. degree, see Andrew Clark, Register of the University of Oxford (Oxford, 1887), II, i, 21-66. The statutory residence requirement was sixteen terms. When Gosson was admitted B.A., he had completed only fifteen terms; but if he had remained in residence until the determination exercises in the following Lent, he would have completed the required sixteen.

21. Clark, Register, I, iii, 62.

succeeding Lent (1577) and go through the formal ceremony of
determination. But there is no record to show that he did so,
and he later signed himself only "Stud. Oxon.," not "B.A."
Something happened to prevent him from completing his degree.
It is quite evident that he had planned for himself a
scholar's career with continued residence in his college, and
that he left the University by no will of his own. His
Ephemerides of Phialo is an undisguised plea to Sidney to
get him a scholar's place at court, or to provide him with
means to return to Oxford and resume his studies; and in his
Playes Confuted (fol. G7^v, p. 217) he complained of being
"pulde from the universitie before I was ripe." The most
probable explanation of his premature departure is that he
was disappointed in his expectations of a fellowship and,
failing that, did not have sufficient money to keep himself
longer at Oxford.[22]

---

22. James Harrison, in his Description of England, ed.
F. J. Furnivall (1877-8), I, 77, complains that it is "an hard
matter for a poore mans child to come by a felowship (though
he be never so good a scholer, and woorthie of that roome.)
Such packing also is used at elections, that not he which best
deserveth, but he that hath most friends, though he be the
woorst scholer, is alwaies surest to speed." John Lyly, who
also seems to have been disappointed in a fellowship and was
likewise forced to turn to his pen for support, wrote in his
Euphues, "Yet may I of all the rest most condemne Oxford of
unkindnes...who seemed to weane me before she brought me
foorth" (Works, I, 325).

CHAPTER II: THE PLAYWRIGHT AND PAMPHLETEER

i

It was apparently early in the year 1577 that Gosson, carrying with him no very good will toward the University that had set him adrift, came to London to seek his fortune.[1] A passage in his Ephemerides of Phialo which, if we substitute Oxford for Siena and London for Ferrara, may be autobiographical, implies that he at first tried to get some kind of patronage. Phialo says:

> After this sorte when my selfe was puld from Sienna,....having nothing...to shore up my studies, I wrote certaine Rapsodia to a Courtier in Ferara, hoping to finde some favour with him, because it was tolde me, that he was learned, but I lost my labour, and at his own request and my charges, daunsed attendaunce certaine daies at the Court, without thankes. (fol. D7ᵛ)

But if Gosson did dance attendance at court, his labor, like Phialo's, was in vain.

There were few other opportunities for making a livelihood open to him. His father had given him an education instead of a trade, so that practically all he was fitted for, outside the court, was a position as tutor in some private family or a place in the Church. But to get places such as these required a patron, special influence of some sort, and even then a long period of waiting until a position offered. Lacking that, his only resource was his pen.

On the basis of an erroneous reference by Francis Meres,[2]

---

1. The date of his admission to the degree of B.A. (December 17) was the last day of Michaelmas term. Christmas term did not begin until January 14, and by that time he had probably already left the University. See his attack on Oxford in the Schoole of Abuse, fols. E2-E3ᵛ, pp. 51-2. For similar attacks by John Lyly, see his Works, ed. R. W. Bond (Oxford, 1902), I, 273-6.

2. See Appendix B, III.

Gosson's previous biographers have assumed that he began his
literary career by writing pastorals. None of these have sur-
vived to our time, for the simple reason that they never existed. But although he did not write pastoral poetry, he was
a versifier of sorts, as what university man was not in those
days? His poems, however, were slight pieces done to order,
commendatory verses to books published by his friends and associates. Perhaps even as a student, certainly within a month
or two of his leaving the University, his first poem, entitled
Speculum humanum, was printed at the end of H. Kirton's translation from Pope Innocent III, The Mirror of Mans lyfe (1576).
It is a pedestrian work, composed by heaping together a series
of lugubrious epithets on the theme that life is "a hugie heape
of bale and miserie." Its only interest is that it shows him
in a typically solemn and didactic mood, and that it justifies
a statement he later made in the Ephemerides:

> Spero me in adolescentiae deliciis cum Poetae
> personam sustinerem, moribus iis enituisse, qui fru-
> gem virtutis nutricarent, et futurae industriae cul-
> mum erigerent. (fol. *6)

There is no evidence that he at any time wrote the kind of poetry he later attacked.
          In February, 1578, he wrote six stanzas of English verse
and twelve lines of Latin elegiacs in praise of Thomas Nicholas's translation from Lopez de Gomara, The Pleasant Historie
of the Conquest of the Weast India, a work which, like Gosson's
own Playes Confuted later, was dedicated to Sir Francis Walsingham. The first stanza of his English poem is curiously
prophetic of the attitude he adopted a year later when he attacked the stage:

> The Poet which sometimes hath trod awry,
> And song in verse the force of fyry love,
> When he beholdes his lute with carefull eye,
> Thinkes on the dumpes that he was wonte to prove.
> His groning spright yprickt with tender ruth,
> Calles then to minde the follies of his youth.

The lines express a commonplace and are designed to illustrate
a comparison developed later in the poem; no autobiographical
reference is intended. But that such a figure should have
suggested itself to him shows something of the tenor of his
thoughts in his supposedly unregenerate youth.
          In August of the same year he contributed a short com-
mendatory poem to John Florio's Firste Fruites. Later, in the

Schoole of Abuse and the Ephemerides, he occasionally gave his
own metrical translations of short passages of Latin verse.
Some of these were in heroic couplets, one in a couplet of four-
teeners, and two in blank verse. This is all the poetry he ever
published. The most that can be said for his work in this kind
is that he knew what a rime was and could count syllables, which
is more than can be said for many of his contemporaries who got
their verses into print.

But no man ever made a living out of lyric poetry during
the reign of Elizabeth. Gosson's few published verses were
pieces done to order and, though they may have brought him some
good will, yielded him little or no financial return. Meanwhile, he had his living to make, so he turned his pen to the
more lucrative, though at that time less respectable, trade of
writing for the commercial stage. None of his plays are extant,
but from his own remarks and the comments of Lodge we can gain
some idea of what they were like.

In the preface to Playes Confuted (1582) Gosson said:

> I was very willing to write at this time, be-
> cause I was enformed by some of you which heard it
> with your eares, that since my publishing the Schole
> of Abuse, two Playes of my making were brought to
> the Stage: the one was a cast of Italian devises,
> called, The Comedie of Captaine Mario: the other
> a Moral, Praise at parting. These they very im-
> pudently affirme to be written by me since I had
> set out my invective against them. I can not denie,
> they were both mine, but they were both penned two
> yeeres at the least before I forsoke them, as by
> their owne friends I am able to prove. (fol. A7-7ᵛ,
> pp. 165-6.)

As the Schoole of Abuse was entered in July, 1579, Captaine
Mario and Praise at Parting must have been written by the
summer of 1577 and sold to some company of actors. As Gosson
appealed only to the players and not to the audiences of the
theaters to prove that "they were both penned two yeeres at
the least before I forsoke them," it is to be assumed that
they were never presented on the stage until the winter of
1581-1582, when they were brought out to discredit the Schoole
of Abuse.

Another of Gosson's productions, which he mentioned in
the Schoole of Abuse as among the few plays presented on the
London stage that did not fall under his censures, was Catilins Conspiracies. Of it he said:

Because it is knowen to be a Pig of myne owne
Sowe, I will speake the lesse of it; onely giving
you to understand, that the whole marke which I shot
at in that woorke, was too showe the rewarde of traytors in <u>Catilin</u>, and the necessary government of
learned <u>men</u>, in the person of <u>Cicero</u>, which forsees
every danger that is likely to happen, and forstalles
it continually ere it take effect. (fol. C7, p. 40)

Lodge, in his <u>Reply to Gosson</u>, remarked:

For the pigg of your owne sow, (as you terme it)
assuredly I must discommend your verdit, tell me
Gosson was all your owne you wrote there: did you
borow nothing of your neyghbours? out of what booke
patched you out Ciceros oration? whence fet you
<u>Catulins invective</u>? Thys is one thing, <u>alienam olet
lucerna, non tuam</u>, so that your helper may wisely
reply upon you with Virgil.
　　　<u>Hos ego versiculos feci tulit alter honores</u>.
I made these verses other bear the name.
beleve me I should preferr Wilsons. Shorte and
sweete if I were judge, a peece surely worthy prayse,
the practise of a good scholler, Would the wiser
would overlooke that, they may perhaps cull some
wisedome out of a players toye. (fols. C5^V-C6)

Lodge was evidently referring to some play, now lost, by Robert
Wilson, the actor and playwright, who since 1562 had been a
member of Leicester's company. The charge of plagiarism comes
strangely from Lodge, especially in a work which he himself
had copied largely from an old schoolbook. In his published
writings Gosson did not draw more from secondary sources than
was condoned by Elizabethan practice. Possibly he had been
engaged to rewrite an old play of Wilson's. In 1598 Wilson
and Henry Chettle were paid by Henslowe for work on a play
entitled "cattelanes consperesey,"[3] which probably represents
still another reworking of the same theme.

---

3. <u>Henslowe's Diary</u>, ed. W. W. Greg (1904-8), I, 94. E.
K. Chambers's assumption in his <u>Elizabethan Stage</u> (Oxford,
1923), III, 516, that Wilson had written a play entitled <u>Short
and Sweet</u> results from a misreading of Lodge's reference quoted above. The expression is proverbial and is intended only
to characterize the play; if it had been meant for a title,
it would have been italicized.

Captaine Mario, Praise at Parting, and Catilins Conspiracies are all of Gosson's plays that we know by title. But if,
as seems likely, the first two were not acted until after the
publication of the Schoole of Abuse, he must have written
others. In his preface to the Schoole of Abuse he said, "Mine
owne woorkes are dayly to be seene upon stages, as sufficient
witnesses of mine owne folly, and severe Judges againste my
selfe" (fol. *6^V, p. 18); and in the preface to his Ephemerides of Phialo he mentioned the accusation of his enemies that "
qui Poetas reprehendo, Poetae partes suscepisse, et dictasse
iis versus quos in Theatris recitarunt" (fol. *6). His use of
the plural in these two passages indicates that more than one
of his plays were at that time being acted. Catilins Conspiracies was one, but there must have been others; the general ten-
or of his remarks implies that there were several others.
There may be a reference to one of these in a passage in Lodge'
Reply:

> Your Muscovian straungers, your Scithian mon-
> sters wonderful, by one Eurus brought upon one
> stage in ships made of Sheepeskins, wyll not prove
> you a poet. (fol. B2^V)

In another passage, replying to Gosson's attack on music, he
says, "It had bene a fitter jest for your howlet in your playe,
then an ornament in your booke" (fol. B6^V).

No other of Gosson's contemporaries have anything to say
about his work as a playwright,[4] which probably indicates that,
although an industrious, he was not a particularly successful
writer for the stage. He admitted himself that he did not
thrive in the profession. This was to be expected, for he had
none of the qualifications that make a good dramatist. His
only narrative, the Ephemerides of Phialo, shows that he was
either uninterested in, or incapable of, plotting and characterization. Like most other plays of the period, his comedies
and tragedies were written in verse--at least, he always referred to them as poetry--and we have already seen his limitations when working in that medium. His aptitude was for controversy and pamphleteering, so that he probably acted wisely
in abandoning the stage when he did.

---

4. J. L. Scott, in his edition of the Letter-Book of
Gabriel Harvey (Camden Society, XXXIII), p. 59, not realizing
that "pig of my own sow" was an ancient and common proverb,
mistakenly assumed that Harvey referred to Catilins Conspiracies when he used the expression.

When Gosson later made an about-face and attacked the
London theaters, he was not at all averse to talking about
his work as a playwright; in fact, he rather boasted of it.
But there was one phase of his career in London about which
he maintained a discreet silence, and that was his personal
appearance on the boards as a performer. Actors were held in
no very high esteem by the Elizabethans--witness Shakespeare's
lament on his "outcast state"--and the odor of the tiring
house ill befitted the odor of sanctity Gosson later assumed.
But Lodge, in his Reply, taunted him with, "I knewe you my
selfe a professed play maker, and a paltry actor" (fol. B8),
and "I shold blush from a player, to become an enviouse preacher" (fol. A4^v), and "your players ornaments...best becam[e]
you" (fol. C3^v). Lodge was an unscrupulous controversialist
and did everything he could to blacken his opponent's character; but if silence means assent, his taunt was true. In
Playes Confuted Gosson carefully answered Lodge's arguments
one by one, but he made no reply to the charge of his having
been an actor.

Most players were enrolled nominally as members of some
nobleman's household, otherwise they were classed as master-
less men and liable to punishment as rogues and vagabonds.
One hint we have as to the company with which Gosson was associated is his statement that his play Catilins Conspiracies
was "usually brought in to the Theater." The balance of evidence favors Leicester's men as the occupants of the Theater
from 1576 until at least 1580,[5] so we may assume that he was
a member of their company. There is one piece of possible
confirmatory evidence for this assumption. Commendatory
verses for a book were usually written by the author's friends
and associates. John Florio, to whose Firste Fruites Gosson
contributed a laudatory poem, dedicated his book to Leicester
and was apparently well acquainted with Leicester's players.
Of the eight other persons contributing commendatory verses,
three signed themselves T. C., I. P., and R. Wilson respec-
tively, which fit perfectly Thomas Clarke, John Perkin, and
Robert Wilson, who were shareholders in Leicester's company.
Two other sets of verses were signed John B. and Ri. T.,
which may stand for John Bentley and Richard Tarlton, both
noted players and poets who, there is also strong reason to
believe, were members of Leicester's company.[6]

---

5. Chambers, Eliz. Stage, II, 393-4. F. G. Fleay's assumption in A Biographical Chronicle of the English Drama (1891),
II, 403, that Gosson wrote for the Chapel Boys company, has
nothing to support it.

Besides Kirton, Nicholas (who had been a merchant in the
Canary Islands), Florio, and the players, we know nothing definite of Gosson's associates in London at this time. He probably knew John Lyly, who was his fellow-townsman and had been
a student with him at Oxford; the two men were at least acquainted with one another's works.[7] Of how he conducted himself we know even less. If we are to believe his enemy Lodge,
who charged him in his Reply with, "Your giddy brain made you
leave your thrift, and your abuses in London some part of your
honestie" (fol. A2), he played the part of a parasite, swagger-
ed in borrowed finery, and frequented bawdy houses. But Lodge,
like other weak contestants, did not scruple to lie about his
opponent's character when he ran out of arguments. Gosson
could scarcely have risen so soon and so rapidly in the Church
if his early life had been as riotous as his enemies made it
out.

ii

Gosson did not prosper in the trade of actor and playwright. Referring to his dramatic activities, he said:

> I gave my self to that exercise in hope to
> thrive but I burnt one candle to seek another, and

---

6. Arundell del Re, in his edition of the Firste Fruites
(Formosa, 1936), II, 8-11, also suggests the actors Wilson and
Tarlton; his other suggestions for identifying the authors of
the commendatory verses differ from mine. Florio had been sup-
porting himself in London since 1576 by giving instruction in
Italian. Frances Yates, in her John Florio (Cambridge, 1934),
p. 51, assumed that Gosson and the other writers of verses for
Firste Fruites were his pupils. But I doubt whether Gosson
could have afforded to pay for lessons; furthermore, there is
evidence (see Chapter VI) to show that at this time he was entirely ignorant of the Italian language.

7. In Euphues and his England Lyly praised Gosson's
Ephemerides of Phialo, which is the only contemporary work he
ever referred to directly (Works, II, 99). Chambers (Eliz.
Stage, III, 412) suggests that Lyly may have been the author
of "the twoo prose Bookes plaied at the Belsavage" which
Gosson praised in the Schoole of Abuse; but this is only a
guess. N. J. Halpin's suggestion, in his Oberon's Vision...a
Comparison with Lylie's Endymion (1843), pp. 74-5, that Lyly
satirized Gosson in the person of Sir Tophas in his Endymion,
has nothing whatever to support it.

lost bothe my time and my travell, when I had done.
(Schoole of Abuse, fol. C7^V, p. 41)

If his character of Phialo in the Ephemerides was meant for a
self-portrait, as I think it was, then we have an even more
explicit statement of his circumstances, for Phialo lamented:

> I shall shortly be dryven too stop bottelles
> with my bookes, and buye me a wallet....And trust
> mee if I thrive no better by my simple travel than
> I have doone yet, I will reverence the Muses as
> longe as I live, but banish them my studie for feare
> of afterclaps. (fol. E6)

Gosson, we hope, was not reduced to begging with his wallet;
but he was led to banish the Muses. Seeing no profit in his
present occupation, he made a resolute about-face and vigorously attacked the theater with which he had so recently been
associated. The immediate result of his action was the publication of a small pamphlet entitled The Schoole of Abuse,
Conteining a pleasaunt invective against Poets, Pipers, Plaiers, Jesters, and such like Caterpillers of a Commonwelth,
which was entered on the Stationers' Register, July 22, 1579,
and dedicated to "the right noble Gentleman, Master Philip
Sidney Esquier."
        The reason for his defection, Gosson would have his read-
ers believe, was a sudden moral reformation:

> Now if any man aske me why my selfe have penned
> Comedyes in time paste, and inveigh so egerly against
> them here, let him knowe that Semel insanivimus om-
> nes: I have sinned, and am sorry for my fault: hee
> runs farre that never turnes, better late than never.
> (fol. C7^V, p. 41; cf. fol. *6^V, p. 18)

The statement was good journalism. The confession of a repent-
ant sinner has always drawn sympathetic attention, and if that
sinner exhorts his listeners to avoid the evils into which he
has fallen, his words carry authority. Other men before Gosson
had attacked the stage; but most of them spoke from hearsay and
prefaced their criticisms with "it hath bene sayd" or "it is
tolde me," so that little notice had been taken of them. However, when Gosson wrote his pamphlet, "my selfe...seeing the
abuses which I reveale, trying them thorowly to my hurt, and
bearing the stench of them yet in my owne nose" (fol. *4^V, p.
17), people listened and were persuaded by his arguments.
        Why it took him almost three years to realize the error

of his ways is another question. Certain bits of evidence
suggest that the writing of the Schoole of Abuse, far from
being the unselfish and public spirited act Gosson pretended
it to be, was actually a piece of hack work done to order,
for which he was generously paid, and that only after he found
he could make no money writing for the stage did he find it
profitable to write against it. Propaganda is not an invention of the twentieth century; the Elizabethan authorities
well knew how to sway public opinion. Walsingham hired university professors to lecture on anti-Catholic divinity,
Burghley dictated political topics for sermons to preachers
at Paul's Cross, the bishops engaged pamphleteers to answer
the Martinists, and even the stage was used for the dissemination of ideas favored by certain groups. About the time
the Schoole of Abuse was published the city fathers were much
annoyed at the conditions in the theaters without the walls
and in the innyards where plays were given inside London itself; but they had been able to accomplish very little in
making the owners of these places correct the abuses which
there flourished. What they needed was to arouse public
opinion against the playing places. Gosson, a poor and dis-
satisfied playwright, and also a scholar and a wit, was just
the man for their purpose.

There are at least six good reasons for believing that
Gosson was hired to write the Schoole of Abuse. First, there
is the manner in which his pamphlet was published. Bibliographical evidence[8] shows that two editions of the Schoole of
Abuse were published in the latter part of 1579 within a very
short time of one another, and that the copies of the first
edition were made up indiscriminately from two different settings of type. In other words, the first edition was a double
printing which, on the basis of the practice of Elizabethan
stationers, means that something like three thousand copies
of the pamphlet were run off the press before it was published.[9]
Ordinary editions of Elizabethan books averaged only about
five hundred copies. Certainly no stationer would order an
initial printing of three thousand copies of a work by an
entirely unknown author if he were publishing it merely as
an independent business venture. Woodcock, and his printer
Dawson, must have received assurance ahead of time from some
substantial agent that they would be reimbursed for their
charges. The agent probably represented the city authorities,

---

8. See Appendix B, I.
9. R. B. McKerrow, An Introduction to Bibliography
(Oxford, 1928), p. 214.

who ordered a large initial printing in order to insure rapid
and widespread distribution of the pamphlet.

Second, the Mayor and Aldermen also engaged another rene-
gade playwright, Anthony Mundy, to attack the stage. His anonymous A second and third blast of retrait from plaies and Theaters was published in 1580 "by auctoritie," and bore the arms
of the city prominently emblazoned on the back of the title
page. The fact that the Second and third blast referred to the
Schoole of Abuse as the "first blast,"[10] although there had
been earlier pamphlets against the stage, notably Northbrooke's,
suggests that it had some official connection with Gosson's
treatise. In fact, Mundy and Gosson apparently divided the
work of attacking the theaters between them ahead of time,
Gosson "overthrowing their Bulwarkes, by Prophane Writers,
Naturall reason, and common experience;" Mundy, whose "second blast" was a translation from Book VI of Salvian's De
Gubernatione Dei, providing theological arguments and citations from the Church Fathers and the Bible.

Third, when Lodge tried to bring out his reply to the
Schoole of Abuse, "the godly and reverent that had to deale
in the cause, misliking it, forbad the publishing,"[11] which
shows that Gosson had strong support from the licensing authorities. Fourth, the epistle at the end of the Schoole of
Abuse "To the right honorable Sir Richard Pipe, Knight, Lorde
Maior of the Citie of London, and the right worshipful his
brethren," which contained the suggestion that "if their [the
players'] letters of commendations were once stayed, it were
easie for you to overthrowe them" (fol. E8, p. 56), recommended precisely the course of action that the Mayor and Aldermen
had been for some time trying to put into effect. It is significant that Sir Richard Pipe had been a member of the com-
mittee, appointed in April, 1574, to "consider the bill ex-
hibited for playes and players,"[12] that was responsible for
drawing up the Licensing Order of December 6, 1574, and that
the Schoole of Abuse, both in the limitations of its attack
and in what it recommended, closely followed the points laid
down in that Order.

Fifth, the publication of the Schoole of Abuse marked the
turn of Gosson's fortunes. Earlier he had been an impoverish-
ed playwright and actor trying to scrape together a living in
London, afterwards he received a position as tutor in the
country, then probably an appointment as a government agent on

---

10. Ed. W. C. Hazlitt, The English Drama and Stage (1869),
p. 99.

11. An Alarum against Usurers (1584), fol. A3.

12. Malone Society, Collections (Oxford, 1907-31), II, 308.

the Continent, and finally a series of benefices in the Church.
Evidently the writing of this pamphlet gained him friends and
patronage.

Sixth, further confirmation of the hypoethsis that Gosson
was hired to attack the stage comes from a passage discovered
by Professor Knappen in the manuscript collections of Roger
Morrice, who lived in the second half of the seventeenth century. In his notes Morrice observed that in the late 1570's
and early 1580's "the Judges, the Templars, and the Puritans
of all professions and conditions being very sensible how the
youth was alienated from religion and corrupted by cards, dice,
revels, plays, and interludes...many Puritans were engaged to
write against them;" and he specifically listed Gosson with
his Schoole of Abuse as one of the pamphleteers so "engaged."13

But even though Gosson had been hired to write his attack
on the stage, it would not be fair to say that he was insin-
cere in his criticism of the abuses he described. He had been
educated according to principles of strict morality, and he

------

13. Morrice MS. I, fol. 615(6), in Dr. Williams' Library, London, quoted by M. M. Knappen, Tudor Puritanism (Chicago,
1939), p. 439. Professor Knappen has been very generous and
helpful in sending me additional information and comment in
response to my enquiries. He informs me that, from his knowledge of Morrice's methods of collecting information, he would
expect him to have had definite evidence, either from manuscript materials now lost or from oral tradition, for his
statement concerning the engaging of pamphleteers and Gosson's
being among their number. Morrice makes the usual mistake,
common in his time and since, of assuming that everyone who
attacked popular recreations was a Puritan. His account of
the part that the lawyers of the Inns of Court took in the
controversy throws new light on the rapid spread of prejudice
against the drama. However, that Gosson himself was subsi-
dized by the lawyers, rather than by those of other "professions and conditions" mentioned by Morrice, does not seem
likely. His epistle in Playes Confuted to "the Rightworshipful Gentlemen and students, of both universities, and the
Innes of Court" contains no statement to show that he had received any support from them; indeed, he appears to be uncertain about the kind of reception they will give his pamphlet, saying: "What effect my labour wil take among you, I
am not sure" (fol. A6^v, p. 165). The general tone of his epistle rather sounds as if he expected opposition from them. It
may be noted that Lodge, at the time of writing his Reply to
Gosson, was a student in Lincoln's Inn.

must have been shocked from the very beginning by conditions
in the Elizabethan playhouses. There was nothing inconsistent
in his opposition to the stage. His only inconsistency was in
forming a connection with it in the first place. This, I have
shown, was the result rather of an accident of fortune than of
any deliberate choice of his own. He had been driven into the
profession of a playwright by poverty, and soon regretted the
step which necessity had forced him to take. If we may believe
his own protestations, he had attempted a reform from within by
writing plays that were "without rebuke;" but he saw "such a
Gordians knot of disorder in every play house," that he finally
realized a direct attack was necessary.[14] Perhaps without sub-
vention he would not have gone so far as to attack the theater
in print; but that he was looking for other fields for his talents even before publishing the Schoole of Abuse, is shown by
his Ephemerides of Phialo.
        Discussion of the part Gosson played in the anti-stage
controversy is reserved for Chapter IV; but in the Schoole of
Abuse he did not confine himself to attacking the stage alone.
His essay grew under his hands until it became, like Stubbes's
Anatomie of Abuses, an invective against most of the social
evils of his time. Excluding the prefatory and concluding e-
pistles, as originally printed the Schoole of Abuse contained
seventy-three pages. Of these, twelve were devoted to an attack on poetry, eight to music, twenty-eight to plays, and the
rest were taken up with miscellaneous reflections, and criticisms of "Fencers, Dycers, Dauncers, Tumblers, Carders, and
Bowlers." His objections to these recreations were that they
corrupted morals, wasted time, and involved a profitless spend-
ing of money. His criticisms typified the attitude of the members of the Elizabethan middle class, who considered the three
cardinal virtues to be honesty, industry, and thrift. The same
prudential morality was upheld by the middle class in later
centuries, and will be found expressed in Defoe's Complete English Tradesman, pictured in Hogarth's Industrious Apprentice,
and exemplified in Franklin's Poor Richard. Typical of this
attitude are his remarks on bowling alleys, which he charac-
terizes as:

        Privy Mothes, that eate uppe the credite of many
        idle Citizens: whose gaynes at home, are not able to
        weighe downe theyr losses abroade, whose Shoppes are
        so farre from maintaining their play, that their Wives

14. Schoole of Abuse fol. C6^v, p. 40; Playes Confuted,
fol. B, p. 167.

> and Children cry out for bread, and go to bedde
> supperlesse ofte in the yeare. (fol. D4, p. 45)

Obviously his objections are social and economic, rather than
religious or moral.

His admiration for the virtues of diligence and industry
led him to a digression in praise of old England, when men had
not been made effeminate by easy living and pleasant pastimes.
Like many of his contemporaries, he believed that Englishmen,
as a result of their country's long peace and remarkable commercial prosperity, were growing soft and losing the virtues
that had formerly made them strong to resist enemies at home
and abroad. "It behooveth us in the meane season, not to
stick in the myre, and gape for succour...or to lye wallowing
like Lubbers in the Ship of the common wealth, crying Lord,
Lord, when wee see the vessel toyle...From the head to the
foote, from the top to the toe, there should nothing be vaine,
no body idle" (fols. E^V-E2, pp. 50-1). For similar reasons he
disapproved of the leisurely pursuit of knowledge merely for
its own sake in academic circles, and denounced those who "in
a close study in the University coope themselves up fortie
yeres togither studying all thinges, and professe nothing"
(fol. E2^V, p. 51). "Season us a little with the Salt of your
knowledge," he admonished them, "thunder in words, and glister
in works" (fol. E3^V, pp. 52-3).

Turning his attention to international affairs, he said,
"Our enimies...have already eaten us with bread, and licked up
our blood in a cup of wine" (fol. E, p. 50), a reference to
the machinations of the Roman Catholics against England. "Have
an eye to the cloude that comes from the South, and threaten-
eth raine" (fol. D8^V, p. 50), he warned; the cloud, of course,
was Spain. Aside from some slight difficulties with France
early in her reign, ever since Elizabeth had mounted the throne
England had remained at peace; but there were many who were
alarmed at the political situation on the Continent. The war
party, composed of men like the Earl of Leicester and Walsingham, urged that the only hope of the country's safety lay in
direct intervention on behalf of the Protestant countries in
Europe and greater military preparedness at home. Sidney was
of the same opinion, and if he liked nothing else in the
Schoole of Abuse, he certainly approved of its militaristic
passages. But though Gosson was an advocate of preparation
for war and consequently held soldiers in high respect, he
had nothing but contempt for the gentlemen duellists of his
time, a social type that was just coming into prominence,
swaggering Tybalts who "thinke themselves...no men, if for
stirring of a strawe, they proove not their valure uppon some

bodyes fleshe" (fol. D5, p. 46). His objections were that
their activities were merely selfish and ornamental, not useful.

In his criticisms Gosson reveals himself as a militant
Protestant nationalist. He did not disapprove of the pleasant
things of life, though he was serious-minded and preferred to
have delight blended in some way with profit. His standards
of judgment were essentially utilitarian:

> No man is borne to seeke private profite: parte
> for his countrie, parte for his friendes, parte for
> himselfe. The foole that comes into a fayre Garden,
> likes the beawtie of flowers, and stickes them in his
> Cap: the Phisition considereth their nature, and
> puttes them into the potte: in the one they wither
> without profite; in the other they serve to the
> health of the bodie: He that readeth good writers,
> and pickes out their flowers for his owne nose, is
> lyke a foole; hee that preferreth their vertue be-
> fore their sweet smel is a good Phisition. (fol.
> E2^V, pp. 51-2)

iii

The Schoole of Abuse had been entered on the Stationers'
Register on July 22, 1579; but probably even before he had begun the composition of that pamphlet, Gosson had started to
write a work of prose fiction entitled the Ephemerides of Phialo, which was entered on the Stationers' Register November 7
of the same year. That it was already in process of composition when the Schoole of Abuse was printed is shown by his
statement to the "Gentlewomen Citizens of London" in closing
the latter work: "Shortely I hope to send out the Ephemerides
of Phialo, by whom (if I see you accept this) I wil give you
one dish for your owne tooth" (fol. F4^V, p. 61). That it was
begun earlier than his attack on the stage is shown by the fact
that there are illustrative details in the Schoole of Abuse
that are drawn from works he had consulted in order to write
the Ephemerides, but which there is no reason for his having
read in preparing his "plesaunt invective." Furthermore, the
style of the Ephemerides is more finished and elaborate than
the style of his first published work, which indicates that
the Schoole of Abuse was written in a great hurry, but that
he had the Ephemerides by him a considerable time with ample
leisure to correct and polish it.

The occasion of Gosson's turning from the field of the
drama to that of the novel was the publication, during the

Christmas season of 1578, of John Lyly's Euphues, the Anatomy
of Wyt. This work inaugurated a new type of English fiction,
a combination of narrative and declamation couched in a highly schematic prose, that became immediately and tremendously
popular, so that Gosson, who was not thriving in the theater,
apparently decided to capitalize on the vogue it had started.
However, he did not set out merely to imitate the Anatomy of
Wyt, but designed his Ephemerides as a reply to the first
part of that work. The name of his hero, Phialo, he probably
took from the passage attacking Oxford in Euphues, in which
Lyly accused "the Philo in Athens" (i.e. the philosophers, or
students, in Oxford) of putting their learning to unprofitable
use instead of employing it in good works.[15] Certainly the
portrait of Phialo, who applied all his knowledge to "reforming of manners" (fol. A8^V) and was wise as well as witty, is
directly opposed to that of young Euphues, who "followed un-
brideled affection" and was a "younge gallant, of more wit...
then wisdome."[16]

But if the characters of Phialo and Euphues are opposed,
the respective works of which they are titular heroes have
many points in common. Both are written in the new Euphuistic
style that had been introduced by Rainolds at Oxford, in both
a slight narrative framework holds together a series of essays
or orations on various topics, and in both the material contained in the formal speeches of the characters is of more
importance than their actions. Gosson, however, remains entirely objective and reports only the words the characters
address to one another; Lyly varies his presentation by reporting sometimes conversation, sometimes set speeches, sometimes the thoughts of characters by means of soliloquies, and
sometimes their ideas as expressed in personal letters.

The narrative portion of the Ephemerides, like that of
the Anatomy of Wyt, can be summarized in a very few words:
Phialo, a young student in the university at Siena, is cheated
of his inheritance and, having no money with which to continue
his studies, retires to Venice. There he meets a former friend,
a young courtier named Philotimo, who upbraids him for abandoning his studies; but after Phialo explains his financial situation and gives him a lecture on the proper method of rebuking
a friend, Philotimo takes him to his lodgings where they spend
the evening in conversation. The next day the two friends

---

15. Lyly, Works, I, 275.
16. Ibid., I, 185, 184. At the end of the Anatomy, however, Euphues reformed and became quite as much a model of
virtue as Phialo.

visit a gentleman named Jeraldi, to whom Phialo speaks at
length on the qualifications of a courtier. In the afternoon
they go sightseeing and Philotimo catches sight of a beautiful
woman with whom he immediately falls in love. Jeraldi tells
him that she is a lady of questionable virtue named Polyphile.
The third day Jeraldi invites the two friends and Polyphile to
his house, where they indulge in lengthy speeches on the subject of Polyphile's hedonistic opinions. Phialo speaks so
eloquently in praise of virtue that Polyphile confesses her-
self converted from her loose ways of living, while Jeraldi
and Philotimo are so taken with his skill in disputing that
they promise to get him patronage at court so that he can
continue his studies.

This is the outline of the plot of Gosson's book, if it
can be said to have a plot. The story has no setting; Siena
and Venice are no more than names. There is no portrayal of
character; the persons are abstractions, as their names signify. There is little action, for nothing of interest ever
happens at the daily meetings of the friends. There is hardly any dialogue; most of the work is taken up with long set
speeches. The narrative portion of the book is indeed the
least important part of it, and was so regarded by the author.
At the end of the second section, when Phialo and Philotimo
take leave of Jeraldi for the night, Gosson remarks:

> What eyther Jeraldi did in theyr absence or
> they when they were returned too theyr lodging, is
> the leaste parte of my meanyng too touche, because
> I have taken this onely upon me, too shewe the
> fruite of Phialoes conference among his friendes.
> (fols. G3ᵛ-4)

Though cast in narrative form, the Ephemerides was no romance,
and was not intended for the delectation of frivolous damsels
or courtly gallants who wished to while away idle hours by
reading about lovers' sighs or feats of derring-do. It was a
serious work and a moral work, as were all of Gosson's writings. Lyly wished no more for his Euphues than that it should
find a place on "ladies lappes," but Gosson intended to provide "meate for manly stomackes" (fol. *7ᵛ).

The first book, which contains "A method which he ought
to follow that desireth to rebuke his freend, when he seeth him
swarve: without kindling his choler, or hurting himselfe,"
tells of the meeting of Philotimo and Phialo in Venice, Philotimo's reprimand to Phialo for leaving his studies, and Phialo's
justification of his action and lecture on the proper method of
delivering rebukes. The important section is Phialo's lecture,

which gives reason for classing the Ephemerides with the manuals of correct social conduct, like Guazzo's Civile Conversatione, that were so popular with middle-class Elizabethans. "As our friendes are not to be rebuked when they are pleasaunt, nor when they are dumpish," said Phialo, "so are they not likewise to be touched in Company, nor in Choler, nor Continually, nor in a bravery, nor when our selves are as bad as they" (fol. B4). He explained the reasons for his seven exceptions at length, with a great jingling of syllables and an impressive citation of examples from ancient history and pseudo-history.

But Gosson had another purpose, even beyond exhibiting his literary skill and reforming manners, in writing the Ephemerides. Phialo quite obviously represents Gosson himself, and his adventures shadow forth the poverty and misfortune, the wit, the skill as a disputant, and the scholarly qualifications of his creator. The Ephemerides is thus a cleverly presented plea to Sidney, to whom the dedication was addressed, for assistance in regaining a place in the University. This is especially evident in the second book, "A Canvazado to Courtiers in foure pointes," which is taken up almost entirely with a long discussion by Phialo on the duties and qualifications of a courtier. It is not Castiglione's, but rather Laurence Humphrey's portrait of a prince that Phialo presents.[17] A courtier, he said, ought "to be learned, to be liberall, to abhorre flatterers, and chiefly of all to further Religion" (fol. D2^v); but the point he elaborated most fully was the necessity for liberality:

> I perswade me that all power, all prefermentes, all offices, all the riches of every countrey is locked up in the court as the fittest Treasurie, that every man by service should fetch his desert, and beg the thing there, that hee hath neede of. (fol. D7)

> You may gather how beautiful a thing it is in Courtiers to be liberall, which is one of the pillers of theyr glory. For theyr nobility comes of theyr progenie, their wealth is the harvest of Fortunes flattery, theyr victories are the fruits

17. Though I have noted no specific verbal parallels, there is a striking similarity of ideas between the Ephemerides and Humphrey's Of Nobilitie. Humphrey described the Christian gentleman, as contrasted to Castiglione's courtly gentleman.

of their Souldiers valiancie...But the prayse of a
benefite, the report of curtesie, the glorie that
shineth in the woorkes of mercie, is all their owne,
not left them by their ancestors, nor lent them by
fortune, nor common to other, stil sounding their
renowne with a golden Trumpet, building them up such
Trophees, such Triumphes, such Idols, such Monуments,
as neither wind shal shake, nor wether beat, nor
water rot, nor fire consume, nor Foes deface, nor
force diminish, nor clowds darken, nor time it self
shalbe able to devour. (fols. E7ᵛ-E8)

It is not difficult to guess what Gosson hoped Sidney's re-
action would be to all this.

In the third book, "The defence of the Curtezan, and her
overthrowe," Polyphile, whose beauty had been praised by
Philotimo, seeks to justify her loose living by arguing that
pleasure is the highest good. "No man which hath any wit,"
she said, "seeing all vertues, al arts, al actions of this
lyfe amed at pleasure, as theyr end, the world made to main-
tene it, every part of the body to desire it, and nature her
selfe too abhorre the contrary, can deny a life so led, to
enjoy perfect happinesse" (fol. H5). This gave Phialo an
opportunity to display his knowledge of philosophy and to
refute her argument by proving that virtue and not pleasure
is the highest good (fol. I3), and to display his knowledge
of theology by showing that man belongs not to himself but
to God: "You are not your owne, but his that framed you; yf
you be not your owne, deny your selfe; yf you be Gods, flie
unto him; cast of the wanton desires of this life, seeke for
no pleasure in these dayes, if you wish to avoid torment in
the worlde to come" (fol. K5ᵛ). "My selfe have alwayes beene
so affected to pleasure," Phialo said, "that I have judged
the daunces of Venus schoole, to be as dangerous as the Mer-
maides songs, which draw us from the coast we are bound to
seeke" (fol. Kᵛ). Phialo's views, perhaps because of the
exigencies of his argument, were more strict and severe than
those Gosson expressed in his own person in his other writings. "For my parte," he said in the Schoole of Abuse, "I
am neither so fonde a Phisition, nor so bad a Cooke, but I
can allowe my patient a cup of wine to meales, although it
be hotte; and pleasaunt sauces to drive downe his meate, if
his stomake bee queasie" (fol. B5ᵛ, p. 31).

iv

Gosson, like Phialo, wanted to get some sort of patron-

age, and to gain this he dedicated both the Schoole of Abuse
and the Ephemerides to Philip Sidney, a young courtier who was
just beginning to distinguish himself. But by 1579 Sidney had
already written several poems; had started work on a prose
romance, the Arcadia; and had probably composed a pastoral
drama, the May Lady. Gosson, therefore, had the misfortune to
dedicate an "invective against Poets...Plaiers...and such like
Caterpillers of a Commonwelth" to a man who was himself a poet
and a playwright. Consequently, scholars in the recent past
have charged him with "stupidity" and "impertinence," and have
called him a variety of uncomplimentary names.[18]

But Gosson was an intelligent, not a stupid, man; he hoped
for a reward of some kind for his dedication, so he did his
best to avoid any impertinence. From our present knowledge of
Sidney's whole career, it is obvious that he would not sympa-
thize with an attack on poetry; but the information that we now
have concerning his character and interests was available to
only a very few of his contemporaries. Sidney did not aspire
to the reputation of a man of letters; he wrote his poems and
prose works only for the amusement of himself, his family, and
his closest friends. None of his works appeared in print until
some time after his death, and the earliest published reference
to his literary activities dates from the summer of 1580;[19]
before that time only a very few of his intimates were aware
of his interest in belles lettres. He apparently even kept
his work as a poet and a writer of fiction hidden from Hubert
Languet, his close friend and trusted adviser.

The kind of book that Sidney's contemporaries in general
thought would attract him can be seen in the three works that
had been dedicated to him before the Schoole of Abuse: Henri

---

18. Phoebe Sheavyn, The Literary Profession in the Elizabethan Age (Manchester, 1909), p. 34; Mona Wilson, Sir Philip
Sidney (London, 1931), p. 156; A. H. Bill, Astrophel (New York,
1937), p. 195.

19. Edmund Spenser, in his letters to Gabriel Harvey that
were printed about June, 1580, referred to the experiments that
were being made by Sidney and Dyer with quantitative meters.
Earlier, in a laudatory poem addressed to Sidney that was printed in Gratulationum Valdinensium Libri Quatuor (September,
1578), Harvey referred to him as one "in quibus ipsae habitent
Musae, dominetur Apollo" (fol. K3^v); but then he also endowed
him with the talents represented by all the rest of the pan-
theon, so that his statements can have no more particular
significance than that Sidney had been born with exceptional
natural gifts.

Estienne's edition of the New Testament in Greek (1576), Theo-
philus Banosius's edition of Petri Rami...Commentariorum de
Religione Christiana, Libri quatuor (1577), and John Stell's
edition of Marnix's The Bee hive of the Romishe Churche (April
15, 1579). Banosius concluded his dedication with these
words:

> Hoc unum precor, ut quemadmodum Alexander Magnus
> Iliadem Homeri, Carolus V. Philippum Cominaeum ad res
> bellicas et politicas feliciter peragendas summo loco
> habuerunt: sic tu Biblia sacra, et doctorum, hominum
> ad pietatem instituta quotidie evolvito, ex quibus
> non tantum prudentior, sed fortior et melior effi-
> cieris.

It is obvious that anyone who knew Sidney only by reputation in
1579 had every reason to expect that he would find a work like
the Schoole of Abuse highly acceptable.

However, Sidney's public reputation and private interests
were at that time somewhat at variance, and he did not appre-
ciate Gosson's dedication. We have it on the authority of
Edmund Spenser that the author of the Schoole of Abuse "was
for his labor scorned;"[20] though apparently Sidney did not at
first choose to express his disapproval to the author himself,
and merely ignored the dedication. Gosson, ignorant of how
his first work had been received but hoping for the best, shot
a second arrow to find the first and three months after the
publication of the Schoole of Abuse also dedicated his Ephemerides to Sidney. He probably did not become fully aware of the
great mistake he had made in the choice of a patron until the
publication of the Spenser-Harvey correspondence in the summer
of 1580.

Meanwhile, receiving no response to his bid for patronage,
he cast about for other means of support. In his Reply (probably written in the late summer or early autumn of 1579) Lodge
taunted him with, "The worlde shames to see you, or els you
are afrayde to shew your selfe" (fol. A5^V). In Playes Confuted (April, 1582) Gosson explained his absence by saying that,
after publishing the Schoole of Abuse, "I departed from the

---

20. Two Other, very commendable Letters (1580), fol. G3^V;
letter to Harvey dated from Leicester House, 5 and 16 October,
1579. That Sidney's scorn for Gosson later became generally
known may be deduced from the fact that Lodge's Alarum (1584),
which contained a violent attack on Gosson, was dedicated to
Sir Philip.

City of London, and bestowed my time in teaching yong Gentlemen in the Countrie, where I continue with a very worshipfull Gentleman, and reade to his sonnes in his owne house" (fol. A8, p. 166). In the epistle to his Alarum against Usurers (entered on the Stationers' Register in November, 1583; but dated 1584 on the title page, which shows that it was published after March 25 of that year) Lodge repeated his taunt by saying that Gosson had "plaid bo peep thus long" (fol. A3ᵛ), in other words, that he was still absent from London. Taken together, these statements show that Gosson was away from the city from some time in the summer or autumn of 1579 until the autumn of 1583, and possibly longer, and that for a considerable part of that time at least he was engaged as a tutor.

He also found himself engaged in controversy. The Schoole of Abuse attracted immediate and widespread attention; and the players, thoroughly aroused by the attack on their profession, hastily marshalled their forces for defense and counter attack. They circulated, in manuscript, a scurrilous personal attack on Gosson entitled Straunge newes out of Affrick; they tried to get someone at Oxford or Cambridge to answer the Schoole of Abuse; failing that, they engaged Thomas Lodge, a young man studying at Lincoln's Inn, to "write certaine Honest excuses, for so they tearme it, to their dishonest abuses" that Gosson had revealed (Apologie, fol. M2ᵛ, p. 73). When he published the Ephemerides of Phialo, Gosson took steps to reply to the players. He devoted the first half-dozen pages of Book I to comments on Straunge newes; he prefaced his work with a Latin letter to the "Literarum Studiosis in Oxoniensi Academia" justifying his action, as a former playwright, in turning against the stage; and he hastily composed a pamphlet of twenty-four pages, An Apologie of the Schoole of Abuse, in which he reaffirmed his earlier arguments, which he had printed and bound at the end of the Ephemerides.

Lodge's Honest excuses, more commonly referred to at present as a Reply to the Schoole of Abuse, was set up in type but suppressed by the authorities before publication. Gosson was not able to obtain a copy until more than a year after its "privy printing." The players continued their counter attacks and, among other things, presented at the Theater in February, 1582, the Play of Playes, in which they attempted once more to refute his charges. This led Gosson to enter the lists again and to issue, in the spring of 1582, Playes Confuted in five Actions, Proving that they are not to be suffred in a Christian common weale, by the waye both the Cavils of THOMAS LODGE, and the PLAY OF PLAYES, written in their defence. The publisher was Thomas Gosson, a London stationer and possibly a distant kinsman of Stephen, who had only recently opened a shop "in Pater noster row at the signe of the Sunne."

Playes Confuted was Gosson's last contribution to the attack on the stage. His pamphlets did at least this much for him, they raised him from comparative obscurity as a not very successful playwright, to a position in the public eye as the central figure in the most considerable literary controversy of the age.

CHAPTER III: THE CLERGYMAN

i

We do not know precisely how long Gosson remained "in the countrie" as a tutor; but in the spring of 1584 we find evidence to show not only that he was absent from London, but that he had left England. The Pilgrim Book of the English Hospital at Rome, under the date April 25 of that year, contains the following entry: "Stephen Gosson, diocese of Canterbury, eight days."[1] The Hospital had been founded in the fourteenth century as a charitable institution for the care of English travelers and undertook to provide, free of charge to any commoner, meat, drink, and lodging for eight days and nights. Since 1580 it had been administered by the Jesuits of the English College at Rome, a seminary devoted to the training of English Catholics for missionary work in their own country; but the Hospital itself was equally open to Catholics and non-Catholics—forty-odd years later the outspoken Protestant John Milton was received there as a guest.

What took Gosson on his foreign travels is a question to which we can only offer guesses as an answer. It may be that the "very worshipfull Gentleman," at whose house he had been a tutor, decided to complete the education of his sons by sending them on a grand tour of the Continent, and that Gosson went along as their governor; but there is no evidence in the Pilgrim Book to show that he was a member of any such party. On the same day that he was admitted to the privileges of the Hospital, six other young Englishmen, three of whom had been students at Oxford, also signed their names in the Pilgrim Book. One of these, Richard Verstegen, was a zealous Catholic who had fled to Antwerp, where he set up in business as a printer and became active in the dissemination of anti-Protestant propaganda. The other five had all been admitted to the English College on April 15 as students preparing for the priesthood; one of them, Richard Blount, worked with such enthusiasm for the cause that he later was made the first Provincial of

---

1. Henry Foley, Records of the English Province of the Society of Jesus (1877-83), VI, 555. I am indebted to Professor Mark Eccles for calling this entry to my attention.

the English Province of the Society of Jesus. Evidently Gosson
had come to Rome, probably by way of Reims, in the company of
a group of young English Catholics who had decided to seek admission to the Jesuit order. Yet all the other evidence at
our disposal shows him as a man of strong Protestant sympathies
and of equally strong anti-Roman Catholic prejudices.

A possible explanation of his presence in such company
may be found in the person of John Cecil, also a former Oxford
student, who had been admitted to the English College with
Gosson's other companions on April 15 and whose name was entered in the Pilgrim Book on April 24. Cecil, even though he
later went so far as to receive holy orders, was actually a
spy and for years kept Walsingham and Lord Burghley informed
of the secret activities of the Catholics. It may be of some
significance to recall here that Anthony Mundy, with whom
Gosson had been associated on the side of the London authorities in the anti-stage controversy, had likewise paid a visit
to the English College at Rome early in 1579, and that on his
return to England, he had used the knowledge gained there to
become a government agent charged with searching out English
Catholics.[2] Sir Francis Walsingham had organized an elaborate
secret service system, and had his personal agents of information in every important city in Europe. Possibly the dedication of Playes Confuted to "one of the principall Secretar-
ies to her excellent Majestie" gained for Gosson a temporary
position as a messenger or a secret agent on the Continent.

The kind of service that such an agent might render is
indicated by the account of how John Rainolds conducted the
divinity lectureship at Oxford, to which he was appointed in
1586. In these lectures, it is reported:

> He grappled with a...renowned champion of the
> Roman church...Father Robert Bellarmine; for his
> subtile head, afterwards graced with a cardinal's
> cap. This Jesuit was then reader to the English
> seminary in Rome; whose dictates, (wonderfully
> favoured,) no sooner taken in writing by his audi-
> tors, but, by some of Secretary Walsingham's in-
> telligencers residing at Rome, they were sent by
> post in packets to the court, and from thence
> speeded to Dr. Reinolds, who, acquainting his audi-
> tory with the very days in every month and week, in
> which Father Robert handled such a point, addressed

2. See Celeste Turner Wright, Anthony Mundy (Berkeley,
1928), Chapters III and VI.

himself immediately to make a punctual answer there-
unto; insomuch that what St. Bernard speaketh to
another purpose, may be truly affirmed of Cardinal
Bellarmine's books of controversies, that they were
prius damnati quam nati, "branded before they were
printed."[3]

ii

Gosson, however, evidently preferred to serve the Church
rather than the Crown, for in the dedication to Playes Confuted
he had renounced profane studies and had promised, "I shall
learne to employ my study to the glory of God" (fol. A2, p.
162). He probably fulfilled his promise after his return from
the Continent sometime in 1584 by taking holy orders. His
first ecclesiastical appointment was as a lecturer--a preacher
without cure of souls on a fixed salary--at St. Martin's
Church, Ludgate.[4]

That he should have climbed "to pulpit from the stage"[5]

---

3. Daniel Featley, "The Life and Death of John Reinolds,"
in Thomas Fuller's Abel Redevivus (1867), II, 225-6.

4. I have not found the record of his ordination. In
his will he left twenty shillings to "the poore of the parish
of St. Martyn Ludgate hill London, where I was also a lecturer
before I was beneficed." There is no mention of Gosson in the
extant records of St. Martin's; but as he was beneficed in October, 1586, and appointed lecturer at St. Dunstan's in February, 1585, he must have taken orders and served at St. Martin's
before the latter date.

5. In the preface to the Percy Society reprint of Pleasant Quippes (1841, p. vii) J. P. Collier suggested that there
was a reference to Gosson in epigram nineteen of William
Gamage's collection entitled Linsie Woolsie (1613):
<blockquote>Is it not strange in this our vain age
To see one clime to pulpit from the stage?</blockquote>
That there is a reference here to Gosson seems to me highly
improbable; for he had left the stage more than thirty years
before Gamage's collection was published, and by 1613 his connection with the theater, if it had not been forgotten, was at
least no longer of contemporary interest. It is more likely
that Gamage had John Marston in mind, for he had been a writer
of plays until about 1608 and then sometime later had abandoned the stage to take orders. Ben Jonson, in his conversations
with Drummond, delivered a somewhat similar quip on him:
"Marston wrott his Father-in-lawes preachings, and his Father-

is not so extraordinary when we consider the character of his
literary works and the circumstances of his education. The
lugubrious theme of his first poem, Speculum humanum; the criticism of frivolous pastimes in his Schoole of Abuse; his warning to "cast of the wanton desires of this life" in the Ephemerides; and even his play, Catilins Conspiracies, with its
didactic purpose to "showe the rewarde of traytors;" all give
evidence of his seriousness and his love of moralizing and
preaching. His education, too, at the cathedral school in
Canterbury and at an Oxford college that had not forgotten the
behest of its founder to cultivate theology, early turned his
interests toward the Church. Almost all his fellow-students
at Corpus eventually held ecclesiastical appointments, so
when he took orders he was merely following the normal and
expected procedure of his former associates.

He evidently distinguished himself in his new profession,
for as the years went by he received a series of preferments,
each more valuable than the last. He had not been long at St.
Martin's when he was given another appointment as lecturer at
St. Dunstan's, Stepney, a rich commercial parish. On February
28, 1584/5, the churchwardens made the following entry in
their minutes.

> At a vestrye holden the day and yeare above
> said by the Cheef of this parishe, Mr. Stephen Gosson
> preacher, being talked withall for serving in this
> parishe as preacher, doth Covenante and promyse that
> on the Wenseday in the forenone everye weeke he wyll
> read a lecture in the Churche and everye sondaye in
> the forenoone he wyll preache and in the afternones
> everye Sonday he wyll Cathachise in the sayd Churche;
> for the which his trayvayle and paynes to be taken
> therin he ys contentyd to accepte the somme of xxx
> pounds by yeare quarterly to be payd That ys to
> saye, at the hands of Mr Cole parson of this paryshe
> the somme of x pounds yearely which the sayd Cole
> hath Convenantyd to paye yearlye as by a byll under
> his hand appearyth, And xx pounds the resydew there-
> of to be paid him at the handes of the Churchewar-
> dens; which the parishe hath grauntyd to Allowe, So
> long as he the sayd Gosson shall Contynew our preach-
> er, this payment to contynew from our lady day next

in-law his Comedies." There were also other playwrights of
the period who became preachers, such as William Gager and
Richard Eedes.

forward Anno 1585.[6]

This contract was duly signed by Gosson, and he apparently began his duties on the following March 25. The parson of St.
Dunstan's, Humphrey Cole, who agreed to contribute ten of the
thirty pounds for his yearly salary, had been his fellow-stu-
dent at Corpus and had graduated B.A. in 1574. Thirty pounds
was a great sum of money in the sixteenth century: players'
hirelings, of which Gosson had been one, were paid only six
shillings a week; skilled artisans could not count on making
much above fifteen pounds a year; and vicars, even of large
churches, not infrequently received no more than that amount.
    His advancement did not stop with his appointment at
Stepney. He had scarcely served six months in his new position when he was presented, October 31, 1586, to the vicarage
of Sandridge in Hertfordshire by Thomas Jennings who held the
advowson.[7] Thomas, and his younger brother John, were sons of
the recently deceased Ralph Jennings of Church in Somerset.
Possibly Ralph was the "very worshipfull Gentleman" to whose
sons Gosson had been tutor. Sandridge is a small parish about
two and a half miles east of St. Albans. In the sixteenth
century the vicarage was rated on the royal books at the yearly value of eight pounds, which means that the gross income of
the living was about eighty pounds. Thus this appointment not
only improved Gosson's circumstances, for to be a beneficed
clergyman on permanent tenure was far preferable to being a
free-lance preacher, but also considerably augmented his income.
    Having an assured position, he returned to London the
next year and married Elizabeth Acton, April 25, 1587, in his
old church of St. Dunstan's.[8] They had two sons, whose bap-
tisms are entered on the Sandridge Register, but of whom no
further record has been found.[9] They also had a daughter,

---

6. Memorials of Stepney Parish, ed. G. W. Hill and W. H.
Frere (Guildford, 1890-91), pp. 9-10.
    7. Richard Newcourt, Repertorium Ecclesiasticum Parochi-
ale Londinense (1708-10), I, 882.
    8. The Marriage Registers of St. Dunstan's, ed. T.
Colyer-Fergusson (Privately Printed, 1898-1901), I, 20.
    9. I am greatly indebted to the Rev. T. A. Talbot-Thomas,
the present vicar of Sandridge, who kindly searched the records
of his parish for information concerning Gosson. To him I owe
the material relating to Gosson's sons, the report of the archdeacon on his preaching, his providing a caliver, and the
transcript of his letter to the archdeacon.

Elizabeth, the place and date of whose birth is unknown. Gosson
seems to have performed his duties conscientiously and well, for
his archdeacon reported in 1588 that he "preached diligently."
He not only preached for his church, he also stood ready to
fight for his country. In 1588 Philip II was planning to conquer England, and on May 20 the Invincible Armada sailed from
Lisbon. Gosson must have taken a grim satisfaction in watching the frenzied preparations to repel the invaders when he
thought of his warning delivered nine years before in the
Schoole of Abuse: "Have an eye to the cloude that comes from
the South...Plough with weapons by your sides, studye with a
booke in one hande, a darte in the other: enjoy peace, with
provision for war." He at least did not fear to follow his
own advice and let "the word and the sword be knit togither."
In May the clergy of St. Albans provided arms and armor for the
defense of the country, and Gosson supplied as his share a
"Calyver furnished," that is, a light musket with its appur-
tenances.
        Fortunately for England, in July the Armada was scattered
by fireships at Calais, storms and sickness took their toll,
and scarcely half the stately ships returned to Spain. Ten
years later Gosson referred to the expedition in a sermon:

        Remember the great Armada in the yeare 1588.
    The preparation was such, that the invader assured
    himselfe of victorie and termed it invincible, yet
    was it in so short time with so few strokes and
    skirmishes, and with so smal ships scattered and
    defeated, that to the eternal memory of gods high
    hand, and the utter scorne and reproach of the in-
    vader there was after the maner of the old Romanes,
    a monument made of it, in certain coyn stamped be-
    yond the seas, with a resemblance of a navie, and
    this word fastned to it, venit, ivit, fuit, it came,
    it went, and it came to nothing. (Trumpet of Warre,
    fol. C3-3ᵛ)

        Though the Armada had been turned back, danger from Spain
still threatened, and the companies of local militia continued
under arms. November 18, 1590, there was a general muster at
Romeland, St. Albans; but Gosson was ill and unable to attend.
He sent the following letter to excuse his absence:

        Mr Archdeacon it hath pleased God to visit me
    with some sickness by reason whereof I am now in
    physic and cannot without danger be at your Court
    to bring in my Armour nothwithstanding I was appoin-

ted a calyver   so I have provided it long since and
have it here at home in my house. Thus desiring
your worship to hold me excused for my absence I
commit you to God. From Sandridge. yours in the
Lord.

                         S. Gosson

     Peace was not made with Spain until 1604. Public senti-
ment veered this way and that, some desiring a treaty at any
cost, others demanding the vigorous continuance of hostilities.
The Queen pursued her usual policy of vacillation and kept her
subjects in perpetual uncertainty. The year 1598 was a particularly anxious time. One correspondent reviewing foreign
affairs remarked, "The remembrance of 1588 makes me fear that
the conjunction of the planets of deceit and treachery then
and now differs little." Early in the year the Spanish fleet
was reported to be outfitting at Lisbon, and foreign intelli-
gencers feared it would attack Dover. The Privy Councilors
were undecided whether to join France and have peace or to
remain by the Low Countires and continue the war.
   ; At this juncture Gosson contributed his bit to the discussion by publishing a sermon he had delivered before the
Mayor and Alderman of London, May 7, 1598, entitled The Trumpet of Warre. "It is a wonder," he said, "to see the base
feare of man, the people of God may sometime be cast into,
when they heare the enimy is in arms" (fol. B).

               Verily the attempts of the enimy uppon this land
          have been many, hitherto your courage and forwardnes
          in the defence of your Country hath encoraged others,
          if you chance at any time to espy the drifts of the
          enimy to encrease, or his rage grow greater and
          greater, be not now apalled, and after so many and
          furious brunts manfully withstood, loose an eternall
          crowne of glory. (fols. E2^v-E3)

Choosing as his text II Chronicles xx: 20, he first discussed
the nature of war, then showed that England's war was charitable and just, and concluded by saying that if the people continued the war they would get from it safety and prosperity in
the end. Thus, just as his early pamphlets against the stage
showed him to be concerned with the morals of his fellow citizens, so this sermon showed him to be also interested in the
politics and statecraft of his country.
     Meanwhile, before this sermon was delivered, Gosson had
taken another step up the ladder of ecclesiastical preferment.
On December 6, 1591, he resigned his living at Sandridge and

was made parson of Great Wigborough in Essex by appointment of the Queen,[10] and here he "contynued parson and resident for the most part of 9 whole yeares."[11]   Great Wigborough is a parish about seven miles from Colchester and has a church dedicated, appropriately for Gosson, to St. Stephen. Newcourt gives the value of the primitiae as eighteen pounds, ten shillings.   In 1610 the rector held "a Parsonage-House with Orchard, Garden, and Yards, two Barns, and one Stable, and about 91 Acres of Glebe; besides Portions of Tyths, lying out of this Parish." Gosson, however, farmed only part of the land and leased the rest to others. As a result, since he had no occasion to use the paths to the fields not in his occupation, the rights-of-way lapsed, and his successor in the living had to bring suit to recover them.

While he was parson of Great Wigborough, Gosson began to gain reputation as a preacher. In the dedication to the Trumpet of Warre (fols. A2-2^v) he remarked that he had been invited several times to address the Mayor and Aldermen of London from the rostrum at Paul's Cross. This was a great honor because only the best and most learned divines of the kingdom were appointed to speak there. Some of the pugnacious spirit he had shown in the pamphleteering days of his youth reappears in his sermons. In a sermon he delivered at Paul's Cross in 1596 he had "stricken at some great person" and was told that he "should be called in question for it." But preaching, he declared, "is haile-shot; we send it among the thickest of you, desirous to hitte you all. And if we can strike, and strike kindly, here a Judge, and there a Magistrate, heere a Nobleman, there a Gentleman, heere a Courtier, there a Countrieman, heere a Lawyer, there a Client, it fareth with us as it did with the Trojans, when the siege was raised, and the

---

10. Newcourt, Repertorium, II, 663. The Rev. F. Yates, the present rector of Great Wigborough, kindly searched the local records for me and reported that all he could find concerning Gosson was that he had transcribed the records of the church in his own hand from the old registers and through the year 1598, and that, October 24, 1593, "Margery Mr Gosson's Mayd" was buried.

11. Public Record Office C24/346/5, a deposition made by Gosson, November 16, 1608, on behalf of his successor at Great Wigborough, Arthur Bright, concerning rights-of-way to certain fields belonging to the living. The deposition was first noticed by C. J. Sisson, Thomas Lodge and Other Elizabethans (Cambridge, U. S., 1933), p. 150; I am indebted to Miss M. O'Farrell for a transcript of the original.

Grecians returned to their ships, they delighted to view the void places where they fought."12

His interest in contemporary affairs, exemplified by his sermon the Trumpet of Warre, preached at Paul's Cross in 1598, has already been referred to. The same sermon contains important testimony concerning his theological opinions, for in it by way of digression he ventured "uppe to the chinne in the Churches quarrell." The main object of his attack was the Puritans, "the new Presbyterie couching downe at the gates of great personnes, with her bellie full of barcking libells to disgrace the persons of the best men, and the labours of the best learned in the Church of England" (fols. E6ᵛ-7). He particularly objected to their controversies concerning ceremonies, the position of the altar, and vestments, for he complained that his day saw "Gods altar invironed with a company of proude Mules, striking at it with their heeles, the altar it selfe battered by violence and beaten downe, holy things troden on and trampled with foule feete...All these miseries springing from a wrangling humor of the Presbyterie, that hath broght religion into contempt" (fols. F3ᵛ-4).

However stern a moralist he might have been, however lacking in consideration for "poets, pipers, players, and such peevish cattel," it is nevertheless evident that, so far as his theological opinions are concerned, he was definitely not a Puritan. For the continental Reformers he had no sympathy whatever:

> By favour and support these Vermine that were long since, by the labours of learned bishoppes hewen in peeces, have crept out of their holes, from Leidon and other places, and by continuall rolling recovered their taile, their torne papers and maimed pamphlets have bin sticht togither againe with a skaine of Sisters thred, and wrought round with a white selvedge of reformation to grace them, whereby the eares of the Church have beene filled with a newe hissing, to the very mockerie of religion, and the impudent slander of the church of Englande. (fol. F3-3ᵛ)

His theological opinions were entirely orthodox, and even in his pamphleteering days he had been an upholder of the Establishment.13 "Puritanism," like "Romanticism," is a word that

---

12. Trumpet of Warre, fols. G5ᵛ-6.
13. See the Ephemerides, fol. F4-4ᵛ.

has been given so many meanings that it is necessary to rede-
fine it every time it appears. Its only unambiguous use is
when applied to the party of reformers, best represented in
its early years by Cartwright, who opposed the government and
ceremonies of the Anglican Church. To call every ascetic or
every moral reformer a "Puritan" is to bring on confusion
worse confounded. There were many Elizabethans like Gosson
who were stern moralists and at the same time gave allegiance
to the Established Church, while on the other hand there were
members of the reforming party who looked with tolerance on
many of the frivolous recreations of the age. Cartwright himself vigorously denied that he and his associates upheld any
peculiar straitness of life.[14]

iii

Gosson's attack on the enemies of the Establishment was
certain to please the Bishop of London, Richard Bancroft, to
whom the sermon was dedicated. Bancroft was leader of the
High Church party and in 1589 had himself delivered a famous
sermon at Paul's Cross which attacked the Puritans, upheld
Episcopacy, established clearly the Anglican position, and
outlined the program which Archbishop Laud later followed.
Gosson explained that he dedicated his work to him "to give
some publike testimonie of my thankeful heart and dutifull
affection to your Lordshippe, which hath enabled me to do
some good in the church of God, in some inferiour services
thereof, according to the talent bestowed uppon me" (fols.
A3v-4). His implication that a superior position would be
appreciated and not undeserved did not go unheeded, for less
than two years afterwards, April 8, 1600, Bancroft rewarded
him with an appointment as rector of St. Botolph's Bishopsgate, London.[15] The living of this church is today the richest in London, and in Gosson's time it was already exceedingly
wealthy, the yearly profits returned for the year 1636 being
three hundred and thirty pounds.

St. Botolph's, which was the Bishopsgate parish church,
stood just outside the city gate "in a fayre Churchyeard, ad-
joyning the Town Ditch upon the very banke thereof...inclosed
with a comely wall of bricks." Nearby was Bedlam Hospital,
and in front of the church was Bishopsgate Street, which ran
through the city from London Bridge to Bishopsgate and out into

---

14. A. F. Scott Pearson, Thomas Cartwright and Elizabethan Puritanism (Cambridge, 1925), p. 89.
15. Newcourt, Repertorium, I, 313.

the fields beyond, where twenty years before Gosson's plays had
been performed at the old Theater. In 1600 the Curtain was
still standing, but the Theater had been torn down and the popular playhouses were now situated across the Thames on the
opposite side of the city. The parish was prosperous and orderly, inhabited for the most part by city merchants and well-
to-do artisans. Here Gosson preached and performed his pastoral duties for twenty-four years. He seems to have gained
the respect and affection of his associates, for the parish
clerk had his son christened Stephen in his honor. He also
was zealous in the care of his church, and in 1620 had the fab-
ric "repair'd and beautify'd" at a cost of more than six hundred pounds.
        The latter part of his life was on the whole uneventful.
Occasionally the marriage of some great nobleman took place in
his church, as that of Archibald Campbell, Earl of Argyll, in
1609. He exchanged letters with Edward Alleyn concerning the
administration of the latter's charities. Alleyn, who had been
born in Bishopsgate, had made a fortune as an actor and theatrical manager. Shortly after the accession of James I he
retired from the stage, bought the manor of Dulwich on which
he founded Dulwich College, acquired a coat of arms, and married the daughter of John Donne. In his letters to him Gosson
signed himself "Your verie lovinge and ancient freend;" but at
that time he had already been rector of St. Botolph's for sixteen years, which is enough to account for the "ancient,"
while "your very loving friend" was a customary form of sub-
scription. Gosson could not have become acquainted with him
in his own acting days, because Alleyn was seven years his
junior and did not become connected with the theater until
1583. Gosson's letters are purely official, dealing with the
appointment of poor boys and superannuated men and women from
the parish as receivers of Alleyn's charity.[16]
        On December 2, 1615, in the sixtieth year of her age,
"Mrs. Elizabeth Gosson, wyfe of Mr. Stephan Gosson, parsone of
this church, was buried in the Quier."[17] Scarcely more than a
year later, March 23, 1616/17, her daughter "Mrs. Elizabeth
Bassano, late wife of Mr. Paule Bassano, gent., and daughter
of Mr. Stephen Gosson," was buried beside her.[18] Gosson was

---

        16. Specimens of the correspondence are given in Appendix
A.
        17. The Registers of St. Botolph, Bishopsgate, ed. A. W.
Cornelius Hallen (Privately Printed, 1889-95), I, 383.
        18. Ibid., I, 387. I have found no record of Elizabeth's
birth or marriage. According to the St. Botolph registers,

left alone with only his maid servant, Mary Judkin, to take
care of him. His two sons, baptized at Sandridge, had probably died, for there is no mention of them in his will. His
sister Dorothy, who had become the wife of William Mansworth,
was far away at Newcastle. His brother William was in attendance at court.

William, too, had come up in the world. We have no information concerning his early career, but in 1599 he was appointed drum player to Queen Elizabeth at the fee of twelve pence a
day. By 1620 he had been advanced to the rank of drum major.
His position at court enabled him to add "gent." to his name
and apparently made him a rich man, for his will, proved after
his death in 1629, specified valuable jewels, household effects,
three houses in St. Bartholomew's, and other property.[19] In
1617 William had gone to Stephen's church in Bishopsgate and
there had become the fourth husband of Faith Towell, the widow
of a London vintner. Stephen appears to have kept on terms of
particular intimacy with his brother, for he left him the greater part of his fortune when he died, and made his step-son,
Anthony Jeffes,[20] the overseer of his will.

Stephen made his will, "beinge in perfecte health of bodye,
and sound sences and perfecte memorye,"[21] November 25, 1622.

"Mrs. Elizabeth Gosson and Mistres Elizabeth Gosson hir daughter" were witnesses at the marriage of the Earl of Argyll in
November, 1609 (I, 44). In that year, therefore, Elizabeth,
though of age, was still unmarried. The baptism of "Elizabeth,
daughter of Mr. Paule Bassano, gent., and Mrs. Elizabeth, his
wife" was recorded April 23, 1616 (I, 198). A second daughter, Anne, was baptized March 17, 1616/17, and buried the next
day (I, 202, 386). Paul Bassanno was probably connected with
the family of that surname whose members had been court musicians since the time of Henry VIII.

19. The documentary material for William's biography is
printed in Appendix A.

20. There was an actor named Anthony Jeffes who was active in his profession from 1597 to 1610; but he could not
have been William's step-son. Apparently there were two men
of that name, and some of the entries in the biographies given
by Chambers (Elizabethan Stage, II, 324) and Edwin Nungezer (A
Dictionary of Actors, New Haven, 1929, p. 203) probably refer,
not to the player, but to the son of Faith Gosson.

21. Collier, in his introduction to the Shakespeare Society edition of the Schoole of Abuse (p. xviii), remarked
that "the papers preserved at Dulwich College in Gosson's handwriting indicate that he was infirm six or seven years before

He left fifty pounds to his sister, Dorothy Mansworth; another
fifty pounds to her daughter; and fifty shillings to "my Cozen
Margaret Oxenbridge." He also left gifts of money, ranging in
value from twenty shillings to five pounds, to the poor of all
the parishes in which he had served—St. Martin's Ludgate,
Stepney, Sandridge, Great Wigborough, and St. Botolph's. Nor
did he forget his associates and helpers, but left small be-
quests to his curate, his maid servant, the parish clerk, and
even to the sexton. The residue of his estate, including his
household goods, he left to his brother William, whom he appointed executor of his will. Finally, he requested that his
body be buried in the chancel of his church, "there to be layd
nere my well beloved wiffe Elizabeth Gosson, and Elizabeth my
daughter." In 1624 the following entry was made in the St.
Botolph's burial register:

> Mr. Stephen Gosson Rector of this parishe for
> 20 odd yeares past who departed this mortall life
> aboute 5 of the clock on friday in the after noone
> beinge the 13th of this moneth And Buried in the
> night the 17. february. [He was aged] 69.[22]

his decease." The only papers preserved are the letters written to Alleyn between 1616 and 1622. In them Gosson's writing
is perfectly clear and firm and shows no signs of weakness
whatever. Collier's remark was probably made to forestall any
criticism of the signature that he forged on the title page of
Pleasant Quippes.

22. Registers, ed. Hallen, I, 408. This entry was first
noticed by a correspondent signing himself E. H., Gentleman's
Magazine, LXV (1795), 750; I have also checked it with the
original manuscript register now in St. Botolph's Church. Fu-
nerals were sometimes held at night to save expense.

i

It was in 1579 that Gosson first attacked the London
theaters in his Scnoole of Abuse, the work by wnich he has
acnieved at least a measure of notoriety if not of fame; and
it is the prominent part he played in tne controversy concerning tne propriety of presenting and attending dramatic performances tnat makes nim of interest to students of Englisn
history and literature. Altnough Antnony Mundy in 1580 referred to tne Scnoole of Abuse as tne "first blast" against
plays and tneaters, Gosson was not tne initiator of tne controversy; otners had gatnered arguments and printed invectives
against tne stage a year or more before he left tne playnouse
to attack it. But ne was witnout doubt the popularizer of
the attack, and it was to a considerable extent tnrough nis
influence tnat the social evils fostered by tne new theaters
became a matter of general notice and general concern.
A survey of tne events leading up to and following the
publication of Gosson's pampnlets will show how important a
part he took in tne controversy.[1] This survey falls naturally

---

1. J. P. Collier gave the first extended account of tne
anti-stage controversy in Conversations VIII and IX of nis
Poetical Decameron (Edinburgn, 1820). Tne most comprenensive
discussion is by E. N. S. Tnompson, The Controversy between
tne Puritans and tne Stage (New Haven, 1903). J. Dover Wilson's
"Tne Puritan Attack upon the Stage," Cambridge History of
Englisn Literature, VI (New York, 1910), 421-61, is a good
short summary containing some new material. E. K. Cnambers,
Tne Elizabethan Stage (Oxford, 1923), gives in every way the
best cnronicle of the controversy in Cnaps. VIII and IX, and
reprints tne more important passages from critical and legal
documents and pampnlets in Appendices C and D. Additional manuscript material concerning legislation is printed in the Malone
Society Collections (Oxford, 1907-31). Several of the more
important documents and pampnlets were reprinted entire by W. C.
Hazlitt, The English Drama and Stage (London, 1869). Virginia
C. Gildersleeve, Government Regulation of tne Elizabethan Drama
(New York, 1908), gives a good analysis of the part taken by

into three chronological divisions: (1) from the beginning of Queen Elizabeth's reign to 1577, (2) from 1577 through 1579, and (3) from 1580 through 1584.

From the time of the earliest dramatic performances to the present there have always been some people who objected to them. Plato expelled the tragedians from his ideal state, the Church Fathers inveighed against the demoralized performances in the Roman amphitheaters, and in the late Middle Ages criticism was leveled at the miracles and mysteries. At some periods this criticism reached considerable proportions, at others it was insignificant; but at no time when the drama existed was it entirely absent. During the greater part of the first eight decades of the sixteenth century a few Englishmen can be found who opposed the drama; but their number was negligible, and their feeble criticism was effectively overwhelmed by the comparatively larger number who praised it. At this time public opinion either was indifferent or was positively favorable to the art of the actor and playwright. When Gosson came to London early in 1577, the attack on the stage had not yet begun.

Several historians of the controversy uphold a different view. They say that sentiment against the stage gradually increased as the century progressed, and they date the actual outbreak of hostilities early, in 1574 or even in 1564. I have analysed the available evidence and have given my reasons for disagreeing with this interpretation in a separate article.

---

the authorities. N. S. Symmes, in Les Débuts de la Critique Dramatique en Angleterre (Paris, 1903), deals with the subject as it relates to principles of dramatic criticism. For the general intellectual and cultural background of the controversy Louis B. Wright's Middle-Class Culture in Elizabethan England (Chapel Hill, 1935) is indispensable. The paper by Charles Cullen, "Puritanism and the Stage," Proceedings of the Royal Philosophical Society of Glasgow, XLIII (1912), 153-81, contains no new material. T. S. Graves's article, "Notes on Puritanism and the Stage," SP, XVIII (1921), 141-69, deals for the most part with the Commonwealth and Restoration periods. The following pages, besides taking into consideration the contents of the above works, also contain a considerable amount of material that was unknown to previous investigators—see the comments quoted from Clement, Fleming, Lupton, Melbancke, Stronge, and Walsal, and from Stockwood's 1579 sermon.

2. "The First Phase of the Elizabethan Attack on the Stage 1558-1579," Huntington Library Quarterly, V (1942), 391-418.

As that contains all the details, and is accessible for reference, it is only necessary here to summarize its argument.
     Examination of the documentary material that has survived
from the first nineteen years of Elizabeth's reign reveals
that comments on the stage, though not numerous, were almost
all favorable. The most exhaustive research has succeeded in
bringing to light only three references that indicate disapproval—one sentence from the two-volume collected works of
Thomas Becon, a short letter from Edmund Grindal, and part of
a single paragraph in a bulky volume by William Alley.[3] These
references are all brief, casual, and in two cases self admitted
to be singular. They are not sufficient to indicate any appreciable hostility to the stage. The prevailing opinion is
typified by the comments of men like the theologian Peter
Martyr and the humanist Roger Ascham. The former said that
plays which are "written honestlye and shamefastlye, so that
they refresh the mind with some pleasure, and are also profitable to set forth good maners, are not to be despised."
The latter said that "for the use either of a learned preacher
or a Civill Jentleman," tragedies are "more profitable than
Homer, Pindar, Virgill and Horace: yea comparable in myne
opinion, with the doctrine of Aristotle, Plato and Xenophon."[4]
     The clergymen at this time saw nothing objectionable in
the drama; several of them were playwrights themselves, and
some even permitted performances in their churches after the
service on Sundays. The attitude of the legislators was
similarly favorable. The Queen and her Privy Council were
active champions of the actors, and the London authorities,
though they banned plays on occasion, did so only to prevent
the spread of infection during a plague and not from any ani-
mosity to the stage. The most important piece of legislation
during this period was the London licensing order of December
6, 1574, which decreed that professional players should have

---

     3. Becon, Workes (1564), Vol. I, sig. BBb2; Grindal,
letter to Sir William Cecil, printed in the Malone Society
Collections, I, 149; Alley, The poore mans Librarie (1571),
fol. 47—the first edition appeared in 1565. Some other
references have been brought forward, but they are not valid
evidence of English opinion on the subject in the period we
are discussing. I have dealt with these in the article referred
to in the preceding note.
     4. Peter Martyr, Commentaries upon Judges (1564), fol.
159^v; Ascham, The Scholemaster [1570], ed. J. E. B. Mayor (1863),
p. 155. For other favorable comments see Symmes, Chaps. II and
III, and Chambers, Appendix C.

the approval of the Lord Mayor and Aldermen before they gave
public performances. This order was only a precautionary
measure designed, not to inhibit playing, but to protect the
welfare of the audiences. Its framers put themselves on
record as bearing no ill will toward the drama, and as making
their regulations in order that all "perilles maie be avoyded
and the lawefull honest and comelye use o plaies pastymes and
recreacions in good sorte onelye permitt ."[5]

The main reason for this lack of opposition to the stage
was that acting and playing had not yet become a social or
legislative problem; and it had not become a problem because
there was very little of it, and because what there was had
still not been commercialized to any great extent. The relatively few references to public performances, and the small
number of plays extant, show that before 1577 dramatic activity
was insignificant when compared with that of the later period,
and that the professional stage played only a slight part in
the lives of ordinary Englishmen. Furthermore, the drama was
still largely a private or community affair. Aside from the
court entertainers, the performances that were open to members
of the middle and lower classes were to a considerable extent
given by amateurs, and the professional actors who depended upon
the general public for support were still a relatively small
and not very well organized group.

But the financial genius of James Burbadge changed all
this by making possible a vast increase in dramatic activity,
which brought the stage into sudden and unfavorable prominence.
The liking of Londoners for public entertainments was obvious
from the crowds that flocked to Paris Garden every Sunday to
see the bear baiting, and Burbadge evidently guessed that
great profits could be gained by making more public entertainment, in the form of stage plays, generally available. In
April, 1576, he leased land in Holywell near Moorfields, already a favorite place of resort for London citizens, on which
he built the Theater, the first building in England designed
especially for dramatic performances. A short time later
ground was broken for the Curtain nearby, and before the end
of 1577 plays were being presented regularly in both buildings.

The construction of the Theater and Curtain in a few
months changed the profession of playing from a small private
enterprise to a big business. Each of the new theaters had
seating capacities that have been estimated at two thousand
or more, far in excess of that of any inn. Also, as they were
designed especially for public performances, plays were given

5. Mal. Soc., Collections, I, 176.

more frequently than before. Earlier it had been customary to
play only on Sundays or holidays; at the Theater and Curtain
performances were at first given three or four or even more
times a week, and later every day. To see a professional play
had, before 1576, been the infrequent privilege of the well-to-
do; after that year even the humblest could regularly attend
plays for a price equivalent, the greater purchasing power of
money at that time being taken into account, to that at present
charged for a moving picture.

The people, rich and poor alike, were quick to patronize
this new form of amusement, and a contemporary writer estimated
that in 1578 the actors in and near London received more than
two thousand pounds a year for admissions to their public performances. As the charge for seeing a play was then only a
penny or twopence, it is probable that more than a quarter of
a million admissions, perhaps as many as half a million, were
sold annually. And this was at a time when the combined
population of London and its suburbs was only 200,000 or less.
So the commercial drama, which before 1577 came only infrequently
into public notice, after that year played a prominent role
among the amusements of a large portion of the populace.

The commercial exploitation and expansion of the public
stage brought about a change both in the nature of the drama
and in the character of its audience. The success of a professional company no longer depended upon getting engagements
to perform before the well-to-do, but upon getting entrance
receipts from the general public. As the object of the actors
at the Theater and Curtain was to get as much money as possible,
whoever paid his penny was admitted. With a mixed crowd in
the pit, disorders were unavoidable, especially as some came
for purposes other than those of watching the players. Young
apprentices ready for riots, cutpurses, courtesans, and amorous
young gallants mingled with sober citizens. As the actors no
longer were confined to performing before a select group, they
had to change their repertoires to amuse this miscellaneous
audience, and so they descended more and more to the production
of frivolous and sensational items which they thought would
have a broad appeal. The new theaters had scarcely been running a year before opposition to them became evident. It was
then that the attack on the stage really began.

ii

In the summer of 1577, when Burbadge's Theater had been
in operation only a few months, an epidemic of the plague, more
severe than any since that of 1563, began in London and continued
through the following year. To prevent the spread of infection,

the Mayor and Aldermen forbade the performance of plays within
the city, and on August 1 the Privy Council issued an order
also prohibiting performances in the suburbs until the end of
September.[6] These were merely the usual precautionary measures;
but in addition, murmurs of disapproval began to come from
certain citizens who viewed with disfavor the kind of plays
that were being given and the kind of audiences that were being
entertained in the new theaters. These murmurs began late in
1577, increased in volume through 1578, and swelled to full
force in 1579.

The earliest piece of evidence for this disapproval is in
A Sermon Preached at Pawles Crosse on Sunday the thirde of
November 1577. in the time of the Plague, by T. W. Imprinted
at London by Francis Coldock. 1578.[7] The sermon was not
entered on the Stationers' Register, but the colophon gives
the date of printing as February 10, 1578 (?1578/79). T. W.,
possibly the Thomas White who later delivered the sermon at
Sir Henry Sidney's funeral, preached on a text from Zephaniah,
"Wo to that abhominable filthie, and cruel city," and asserted
that the London plague was a visitation from God in punishment
for the sins of the citizens. The ninety-eight pages of his
sermon contain a general indictment of the vices of the times:
worldliness, papistry, swearing, profanation of the Sabbath
with merrymaking, covetousness, and luxurious living. In the
course of his argument against Sunday amusements, in which
among other things he reprehended going to alehouses and row-
ing on the Thames, he said:

Looke but upon the common playes in London, and see
the multitude that flocketh to them and followeth them:
beholde the sumptuous Theatre houses, a continual monument

---

6. Chambers, Eliz. Stage, IV, 276.
7. J. P. Collier, in the introduction to his edition of
Northbrooke's Treatise (1843), p. xiv, and also H. S. Symmes
(p. 71) and Dover Wilson (p. 435), give the date of T. W.'s
sermon as December 9, 1576. A Sermon Preached at Pawles Crosse
on Sunday the ninth of December. 1576. by T. W. Imprinted at
London by Francis Coldock. 1578, is an entirely separate work
and contains no reference whatever to plays or theaters. Apparently Coldock printed the 1576 and 1577 sermons at the same
time, and in binding some copies mixed the gatherings. In the
Huntington Library copy of the 1577 sermon, gathering B is from
the 1576 sermon. Chambers (Eliz. Stage, IV, 197) reports that
one of the two British Museum copies of the 1577 sermon has
been bound in error with the title-page of the 1576 sermon--
this is what probably mislead Collier.

of Londons prodigalitie and folly. But I understande
they are nowe forbidden bycause of the plague, I like
the pollicye well if it holde still, for a disease is
but bodged or patched up that is not cured in the cause,
and the cause of plagues is sinne, if you looke to it
well: and the cause of sinne are playes: therefore the
cause of plages are playes. Quicquid est causa causa est
causa causati. Shall I reckon up the monstrous birds
that brede in this nest?...more horrible enormities, and
swelling sins are set out by those stages, then every man
thinks for...you can scantly name me a sinne, that by that
sincke is not set a gogge: theft and whoredome: pride
and prodigality: villanie and blasphemie...thou losest
thy selfe that hauntest those scholes of vice, dennes of
Theeves, and Theatres of all leudnesse: and if it be not
suppressed in time, it will make such a Tragedie, that
all London may well mourne. (sig. C8-8ᵛ)

A month later, December 2, 1577, John Northbrooke's A
Treatise wherein Dicing, Dauncing, Vaine playes, or Enterluds,
with other idle pastimes, &c., commonly used on the Sabboth
day, are reproved by the Authoritie of the word of God and
auntient writers was entered on the Stationers' Register. It
was published at London without date by George Bishop, who
issued another edition in 1579. As its title indicates, it
was a Sabbatarian document, concerned with the various activities permissible on the Lord's Day. It is divided into three
sections: (1) against idleness, idle pastimes, and plays;
(2) against dice playing; and (3) against dancing. The attack
on plays, which comes at the end of the first section on idleness, covers about eighteen pages in the original edition,
something less than one-eighth of the entire volume.

Northbrooke was a quotation-monger of some industry who
had already published two books, The poore mans Garden and A
breefe and pithie summe of the Christian Faith, in which he
had gathered the opinions of the Fathers and various other
churchmen on the commonplaces of Christian doctrine. His
Treatise, though composed as a dialogue between Youth and Age,
was likewise in great part a compilation, from Vives's edition
of St. Augustine's De Civitate Dei especially, and from other
early Church Fathers; from encyclopedic collections and dic-
tionaries like Agrippa's De Vanitate Scientiarum, Polydore
Vergil's De Rerum Inventoribus, and Thomas Cooper's Thesaurus;
and from English works like The Institucion of a Gentleman,
Alley's The poore mans Librarie, and Wilson's The Arte of
Rhetorique. He himself indicated the nature of his work when
he said that it was merely "gathered togither," and when he
admitted that his remarks on plays were not his but the sayings

of the Church Fathers (Collier's reprint, pp. 5, 88).

Because of his scissors-and-paste method of composition,
it is difficult to separate Northbrooke's own objections from
the objections raised by the writers whom he copied. He admitted that it would be "too stoicall and precise" to attack
all plays, and so directed his criticism specifically at the
newly-erected commercial playhouses, the Theater and Curtain
(pp. 83, 85). Apparently his personal reasons for disapproval
were that attendance at them was "right prodigalitie," a use
of money which ought to be applied to more worthy and useful
purposes (p. 84); that they had become a "schoole" in which
Satan brought "men and women into his snare of concupiscence
and filthie lustes" (p. 86); and that they competed with the
ministers on Sundays by drawing people from sermons (p. 93).
He called the theaters schools for Satan because of the plays
shown on the one hand, and because of the audiences that
gathered on the other. From plays, he said, people learn
nothing "but that which is fleshye and carnall" (p. 89); and
the "rabblement" which gathers to see them, where men and
women mingle indiscriminately and gaze at one another, makes
it impossible to keep "safe and chaste mindes" (p. 91).

Yet, after all his criticism, he concluded his discussion
by asserting that it was entirely "laweful for a schoolmaster
to practise his schollers to playe comedies," providing they
did not do so "publickly, for profit and gaine of money" (p.
104). In other words, he did not think that there was anything wrong in principle with dramatic representations, he
merely objected to commercial performances in the new theaters.
His Treatise essentially was more a specific attack on the
Theater and Curtain than a general attack on the drama.

Northbrooke's pamphlet was the first work printed in
England in which an attack on the stage was considered of
sufficient importance to merit mention on the title page.
But it apparently attracted no attention at the time of its
original publication. Even the later attackers of the theaters
ignored it--until 1583, when Stubbes copied a few passages
from it in his Anatomie of Abuses. It probably fell still
born from the press because public opinion was not yet prepared
to receive it. Northbrooke himself complained of the apathy
of the legislators, the clergy, and the people. "Great resort
there is daily unto" theaters, and "yet I see little sayd, and
lesse done unto them" (p. 101); the people should be urged to
refrain from attending plays, and yet "the rulers are not onely
negligent and slowe herein to doe, but the preachers are as
dumme to speake and saye in a pulpitte against it" (p. 103).

The playhouses had been closed at the beginning of August,
1577, to prevent the spread of the plague. However, though the

the plague continued, they probably reopened for the Christmas
season and, except for a period of inhibition in November and
December, continued their performances through the following
year. In 1578 several condemnatory references to the theaters
appear, enough to show that public opinion was gradually being
aroused against them. In February Thomas Brasbridge prefaced
his Poore Mans Jewell...a treatise of the Pestilence with some
questions to be asked by the London citizens:

> Let them ask...whether these daily customes of running
> to playes, and enterludes, and to bearebaitinges, aswell
> uppon the Sabboth day, ordeined for the service of God, as
> upon other days appointed for men to worke...doe displease
> God, and provoke him to plague us, or no?

> Let them aske...whether that playes upon the Sundayes
> be godlie exercises, fitte for the sanctification of the
> Sabboth day, or no: unto the which, light persons for
> the most part resorte: where (throughe light communica-
> tion of one with another,) occasion is ministred of
> furtner inconvenience. (sig. B4)

Two months later S. Stronge, in a commendatory poem to Barnaby
Rich's Allarme to England, exhorted his countrymen:

> Do sorte thy selfe from Comedies, and foolish playes of love,
> Lest tragicall and worse perhaps in fine thee chaunce to
>   prove. (sig. **2^V)

And John Florio, illustrating London life and manners in his
Firste Fruites, remarked that "there is much knaverie used at
those Comedies" (sig. A).

> John Stockwood, who had been patronised by Sir Henry Sidney
and who was schoolmaster of Tunbridge, also attacked "the
gorgeous Playing place erected in the Fieldes" in A Sermon
Preached at Paules Crosse on Barthelmew day (August 24). he
regretted that the theaters had been built outside the Liberties,
where the city's authority could be flouted; he disapproved of
the amount of money paid to players; and he especially objected
to actors performing in competition with the ministers on
Sunday: "Wyll not a fylthye playe, wyth the blast of a
Trumpette, sooner call thyther a thousande, than an houres
tolling of a Bell, bring to the Sermon a hundred?" But he did
not utterly condemn the drama; he objected only to the disorders at the theaters, and to playing on Sunday, and concluded:

> I will not here enter this disputation, whether it
> be utterly unlawfull to have any playes, but will onely
> joine in this issue, whether in a Christian common wealth
> they be tolerable on the Lords day.[8]

---

8. Extracts in Chambers, Eliz. Stage, IV, 199-200.

The same objection was advanced in A Sermon Preached at Pauls Crosse by John Walsal, one of the Preachers of Christ his Church in Canterburie. 5. October. 1578: "It hath bene sayd (I trust it be reformed) that vaine plaiers have had about this citie of London farre greater audience, then true preachers" (sig. E5ᵛ).

In the middle of 1578 George Whetstone published a comedy which had never been acted, the Historye of Promos and Cassandra In his dedication, he defended the drama in general, asserting that the gravest men have "from these trifles wonne morallytye, as the Bee suckes honny from weedes." But his defense did not extend to his own country, where the work of "unadvised, and rashe witted wryters, hath brought this commendable exercise into mislike." He objected to the plays being shown in the London theaters for esthetic reasons:

> The Englishman in this quallitie is most vaine, in-
> discreete, and out of order; he fyrst groundes his worke
> on impossibilities; then in three howers ronnes he throwe
> the worlde, marryes, gets Children, makes Children men,
> men to conquer kingdomes, murder Monsters, and bringeth
> Gods from Heaven, and fetcheth Divels from Hel.9

In the first part of 1579 still more expressions of dis-approval appeared in print. Thomas Twyne, in his Phisicke against Fortune, a translation from Petrarch, brought his original up to date by inserting the names of the new theaters in the following passage: "The Curteine or Theater: which two places are well knowen to be enimies to good manners: for looke who goeth thyther evyl, returneth worse."10 A preacher named Spark, in a sermon delivered at Paul's Cross on April 29, called plays and theaters "the nest of the Divel, and sinke of al sinne."11 John Stockwood continued his criticism in A very fruiteful Sermon preched at Paules Crosse the tenth of May last (1579). As this work has so far gone unnoticed by scholars, it may be well to give a fairly full abstract of the six pages (fols. 24-6) written "Against plaies and other vain exercise on the Lordes day."

> And here I cannot but lament the great disorder of
> this honorable citie, wherin, in this cleare light of the
> Gospel, and in the often and vehement outcrying of God
> his Preachers against suche horrible abuses, there are

---

9. Ibid., IV, 201.
10. Ibid., IV, 202.
11. The sermon is not extant, but is known by the reference to it quoted above in Mundy's Second and third blast (ed.
Hazlitt, p. 99).

notwithstanding suffered licentiously too reigne many
detestable exercises and filthie stage playes, which on
the Lordes day robbe him of halfe his service...I am
sure that by divers godly and learned men they have out
of this place often bin cried out against: so that I
verily beleeve that if in Sodom and Gomorrah they had bin
so much spoken against as in this citie, they woulde not
have shewed themselves so slacke in redressing so foule
an evill: the first beginning whereof had his fundation
from no better place then the bottomelesse pit of hell,
nor no better Author or Inventor then the Devil, if anie
credite bee to bee geven unto the best, the most auncient
and most learned Fathers of the Primative Churche, which
shewe that they were firste instituted in the honor of
vile idols, and filthy Gods of the Gentiles. Some of the
Fathers cal them vanity, and others say that the Theaters
on which they were plaied, were erected by the Divel. And
this they speake in the general dislike of them; but what
would they have spoken thinke you, if they had seen the
greate abuse of our playes, which albeit they bee not
made in the honour of Heathen Gods, yet further they not
a little the purpose of the Devill...And whereas they
will alledge that they play not in the time of sermons;
(albeit that bee no reason why they should be suffered
on the Lord his day, which is wholy too bee spent in his
service) yet the people that resorte thither, yf they
will have any convenient place to heare, must be there
before the time of Sermons, and also all the Sermon while
to, which is cause sufficient enough to restraine them.
When God visiteth your citie with the sicknesse, that
they beginne once to die in anie number, then by and by
cometh foorth prohibition to forbid them: but God once
ceasing his heavy hand, and staying his plague among you,
then up agayne goe the billes on every poste, and on this
Sunday, and that Sunday you shall have suche a wanton
matter at suche a place, and such a place, and thither
runne the people thicke and threefolde as they say, so
that you shall have youre Churches in moste places emptie,
when as the Theaters of the Players are as ful as they can
throng.

During the period of a year and a half that we have just
surveyed, attacks on the theaters were made in ten different
printed works, more than three times the number of independent
attacks than had appeared during the preceding nineteen years.
This shows that opposition to the new theaters was beginning
and growing in strength. Then, on July 22, 1579, Gosson's The
Schoole of Abuse, Conteining a pleasaunt invective against

<u>Poets, Pipers, Plaiers, Jesters,</u> and suon like Caterpillers of
<u>a Commonwelth</u> was entered on the Stationers' Register. Its
publication immediately brought the whole controversy into
prominence.

     Gosson's pamphlet attracted attention because he had him-
self been a playwright. The preachers had spoken from hearsay;
but he had tried the abuses he described to his own hurt, and
knew of what he was speaking. That a writer of plays should
turn from the theater in disgust and with remorse of conscience,
was more convincing evidence against it than all the theoretical
arguments or opinions of the ancients that could be alleged in
its disfavor. Gosson's pamphlet also attracted attention because it was a "plesaunt invective." It was written in the
new and much admired Euphuistic style, and was enlivened with
anecdotes which were amusing in themselves as well as illustrative of arguments against the stage. It was witty, forceful, and vigorous, and so was read by gentlemen of pleasure
for its style, as well as by more sober citizens for its moral
teaching. The measure of its popularity is indicated by the
number of editions it went through. Though its first issue
was a double printing, a second edition appeared in the same
year; and as late as 1587 there was still sufficient demand
for it to justify yet another edition. Very few controversial
pamphlets of the time enjoyed so wide a circulation.

     By his phrase the "school of abuse" Gosson referred, not
to the drama, but to the theaters in which it was presented.
He refrained from attacking the arts themselves, and objected
only to the wrong use made of them by players and playwrights.
He inveighed against improper plays; and because they were
usually in verse, he attacked poets; and because performances
were often enlivened with music, he attacked pipers and "suche
peevishe cattel." He began with a discussion of poetry. "The
right use of auncient Poetrie," he said, "was to have the
notable exploytes of woorthy Captaines, the holesome councels
of good fathers, and vertuous lives of predecessors set downe
in numbers" (sig. A7ᵛ, p. 25). But by abusing their art, poets
have become the "fathers of lyes, Pipes of vanitie, and Schooles
of Abuse" (sig. A3, p. 21). And even if some good things are
found in their verses, yet "where hony and gall are mixed, it
will be hard to sever the one from the other" (sig. A2, p. 20).

     He next discussed music. Ancient music, he said, was
used to encourage men to deeds of valor and to teach them the
harmony and order that reigns in the universe. But effeminate
music leads to lewdness of life. When the martial vigor of
ancient melodies is exchanged for the enervating sweetness of
merely pleasing tunes, moral degeneration follows. His chief
objection to the music of his own time was that the instruments

had become complicated and the strains complex. "The _Argives_," he observed, "appointed by their lawes great punishments for such as placed above 7. strings upon any instrument" (sig. B2, p. 27). This is not as blind a following of ancient example as may at first appear. The popular music of Gosson's day, which consisted of simple airs, was being encroached upon by elaborate sets of variations and the complicated structure of madrigals imported from abroad. This development was doubly damned in the eyes of conservative patriots, because it was new and also foreign. John Rainolds had pointed out the evils of the tendency in his lectures at Oxford: "Mutata musica, mutatis moribus."[12]

Poetry, piping, and playing are "all three chayned in linkes of abuse." In theaters the players set abroach "straunge consortes of melody, to tickle the eare; costly apparel, to flatter the sight; effeminate gesture, to ravish the sence; and wanton speache, to whet desire to inordinate lust" (sig. B6ᵛ, p. 32). And even though some of the productions are "good playes and sweete playes...woorthy to bee soung of the Muses" (sig. C7ᵛ, p. 41)--Gosson here makes specific reference to one of his own plays--yet there are few of that kind, and even they should not be shown in miscellaneous public assemblies. A common argument used by the dramatists was that "every man in a play may see his owne faultes, and learne by this glasse, to amende his manners." But Gosson points out that the pleasure given by the performances so temper "the bitternesse of rebukes," and so mitigate "the tartenesse of every taunt," that actually no one is ever reformed. If instruction is wanted, he concludes, there are divines enough to give it (sig. B5ᵛ, p. 31).

However, his main objection is to the disorders of the audiences rather than to the plays themselves. At the theaters gallants entice honest women to wantonness and harlots hold "a generall Market of Bawdrie." "Were not Players the meane, to make these assemblyes, such multitudes wold hardly be drawne in so narowe roome" (sig. C4, p. 37). And yet, after all his criticism, he is willing to allow plays, if the actors can promise that "everye one which comes to buye their Jestes, shall have an honest neighbour" (sig. D3ᵛ, p. 45).

The arguments of the _Schoole of Abuse_ are remarkable for their essential temperance and reasonableness. Gosson attacked abuses, not the arts themselves; and his objections were social and political rather than theological. He said nothing about Sunday performances, indeed had no objection to honest

---

12. _Orationes Duodecim_ (1619), p. 338.

recreation on that or any other day. He deliberately refrained
from quoting the Bible or the works of the Church Fathers. He
restricted himself to arguments based on natural reason and
common experience, and merely gave the players a "volley of
prophane writers to beginne the skirmishe" (sig. D, p. 42).
He approached the whole problem from the point of view of a
practical legislator rather than from that of a theorizing
moralist.

"The whole body of the common wealth" should "consist of
fellow laborers, all generally serving one head, and particularly following their trade, without repining. From the head
to the foote...there should nothing be vaine, no body idle"
(sig. E2, p. 51). He looked back upon the events of the past
and saw that the abuse of the arts was indissolubly connected
with the fall of empires: "When Rome was a sleepe, the French
men gave a sharpe assaulte too the Capitoll; when the Jewes
were idle, their walles were rased, and the Romans entred:
when the Chaldees were sporting, Babylon was sacked" (sig. D7^v,
p. 48). He looked back to former days in England, when the
exercises of both men and women were "shootyng and darting,
running and wrestling, and trying such maisteries, as eyther
consisted in swiftnesse of feete, agilitie of body, strength
of armes, or Martiall discipline. But the exercise that is
nowe among us, is banqueting, playing, pipyng, and dauncing,
and all suche delightes as may win us to pleasure, or rocke us
a sleepe" (sig. B8^v, p. 34). It was because poets, pipers,
and players were "effeminate writers, unprofitable members,
and utter enimies to vertue" (sig. A3, p. 20), and so menaced
the welfare of the state, that Gosson, like Plato, wished to
banish them. The right use of the arts, he said, was praiseworthy; but in his day they were abused, and it was better
to be without them than to suffer their inconveniences.

The players had been able to ignore the pious exhortations
directed against them from Paul's Cross, and the passing
criticisms made in printed books; but the rapier thrusts of
Gosson's invective pierced the armor of their indifference and
drove them into action. So far as is known, the Schoole of
Abuse was the first attack on the stage to draw a reply from
those who favored the drama.

The players' first move was to attempt intimidation by
threatening Gosson with personal reprisals. In the dedicatory
epistle of his Ephemerides he remarked that "it hath beene my
fortune to beare sayle in a storme, since my first publishing
the Schoole of Abuse, and to bee tossed by such as fome without reason, and threaten me death without a cause" (sig. *3).
Their second move was to attempt to undermine his arguments
by blackening his character. In the Latin letter to the stu-

dents of Oxford, prefacing the _Ephemerides_, Gosson said:

> Aliquot iam menses sunt elapsi, cum ego in Poetárum,
> Fidicinum atque Histrionum ineptias graviter invenebam,
> quo negotio, quia profligatis hominibus in Epicureorum
> hortulis apricantibus, Solem ac Coelum interclusi, mei
> nominis existimationem effraenate invaserunt. (*5-5ᵛ)

Their third move was to point out that Gosson had been guilty
of doing the very things that he reprehended in others:

> Avide sibi hoc homines famelici arripiunt, me qui
> Poetas reprehendo, Poetae partes suscepisse, et dictasse
> iis versus quos in Theatris recitarunt. (*5ᵛ-6)

This, of course, gave him another opportunity to portray himself as the strayed sheep that had returned to the fold:

> Nos ea studia iuventutis aestu persequi, quae flexu
> aetatis nauseamus, et quae desideria eo temporis flore,
> quasi vere tepefacta pullulant, maturiori iudicio
> circumcidi. (*6ᵛ)

Most of these early attacks on Gosson appear to have been
made by word of mouth,[13] by conversation, or in prologues and
epilogues upon the stage. But one attack, at least, was written
out and circulated in manuscript. In the _Ephemerides_ Gosson
tells how a friend of his not long since had presented him with
"straunge newes out of _Affrick_," and had asked him to prepare
an answer to it. After he "unfolded the paper," he found
"nothing within but guttes and garbage" (sig. A). Scholars
have always assumed that Straunge newes out of Affrick was a
printed pamphlet, though no trace of such a publication has
ever been found. But if it had been a printed work, Gosson
would have spoken of opening the book or turning the pages;
instead, he said that he "unfolded the paper." This phrase
clearly shows that he was reading a manuscript.

The anonymous author of this manuscript apparently made
no attempt to answer Gosson's arguments with other arguments;
but relied instead upon personal invective and scurrility:

> This Doctour of Affrike with a straunge kinde of
> style begins to write thus: To his frinds the Plaiers,
> and to win eare...breathes out this oracle...Affrica
> semper aliquid apportat novi...To which principle when
> he thinketh he hath given sufficient light...with a tale
> of a tub, he slippeth down presently into a dirtie

---

13. Further evidence of this whispering campaign is found
in Lodge's _Reply_, which states that Gosson's attack on poets
"hath brought such a sort of wondering birds about your eares,
as I feare me will chatter you out of your Ivey bush" (sig.
A5ᵛ).

comparison of a dutch Mule and an english mare, that ingendred an Asse. (sig. A^v-2)

Gosson replied to his detractors, as I have shown above,
in the Latin letter to the Oxford students prefixed to the
Ephemerides, and in the beginning of that work itself. The
three orations which compose the Ephemerides and the prefatory
letters were probably already set up in type, when he heard of
another attack being prepared against him. The players,
Gosson said, had tried to hire someone at Oxford or Cambridge
to answer his arguments, but were unsuccessful. Finally they
found a man in London "to write certaine Honest excuses, for
so they tearme it, to their dishonest abuses" which Gosson had
revealed (Apologie, sig. M2^v). This man was Thomas Lodge, a
young Oxford B. A., who in the autumn of 1579 was a student at
Lincoln's Inn.[14]

Neither Gosson nor his friends were able to learn anything
about the contents of the reply that Lodge was preparing; but
it was necessary to steal his thunder. Accordingly, Gosson
hastily put together a short essay, An Apologie of the Schoole
of Abuse, against Poets, Pipers, Players, and their Excusers,
and had it printed at the end of the Ephemerides. The Ephemerides was entered in the Stationers' Register on November 7,
1579, and the composite volume probably appeared in the booksellers' stalls about the same time.

In the Apologie Gosson reaffirmed his main position, modi-
fied some of his objections to avert criticism, and answered
the stock arguments always brought forward by defenders of
poetry and music. He first clearly defined his stand:

> They that are greeved, are Poets, Pipers, and Players:
> the first thinke that I banishe Poetrie, wherein they
> dreame; the second judge, that I condemne Musique, wherein
> they dote; the last proclaime, that I forbid recreation
> to man, wherein you may see, they are starke blinde. He
> that readeth with advise the book which I wrote, shal per-
> ceive that I touche but the abuses of all these. When we
> accuse the Phisition for killing his patient, we finde no
> faulte with the Arte it selfe, but with him that hath

---

14. For the evidence identifying Honest excuses with
Lodge's reply to Gosson, only two copies of which survive, both
without a title page, see J. Dover Wilson, "The Missing Title
of Thomas Lodge's Reply to Gosson's School of Abuse," MLR, III
(1908), 166-8. In the Huntington Library copy of Lodge's reply,
a contemporary has written at the top of the first page:
" [H]eare begineth m^r Lodges replye [t]o Steuen Gosen touchinge
playes."

abused the same. (sig. L2^V)
He then pointed out that poems contain gross errors, great
abuses, and horrible blasphemies. The heathen gods, whom
poets honored, were strumpets and parricides; and by saying
that there are many gods, poets blaspheme the true God. If
we try to defend poets by interpreting their verses allegori-
cally, we admit that they are dissemblers; for in allegory one
thing is said, but something different is meant. He next cited
historical examples to show that ancient musicians were more
skilful than the moderns; but he prudently retreated from his
earlier argument that modern music should be suppressed because
the instruments and tunes departed from ancient standards. He
agreed not to forbid "our new founde instrumentes" provided
that "we handle them as David did, to prayse God; nor bring
them any more into publique Theaters, to please wantons" (sig.
L7).

Finally he took up the subject of plays, and pointed out
that both Lactantius and Cicero had condemned them. Players,
he said, are "the worste, and the daungerousest people in the
world," because they "ransacke our purses by permission," and
wound our souls by making evil actions pleasing. One should
prefer "rather to bee a Londoners hounde then his apprentice,
bicause hee rateth his dogge, for wallowing in carrion; but
rebukes not his servaunt for resorting to playes" (sigs. L7^V-
8^V).

The Apologie was cleverly contrived, and effectively
answered most of Lodge's arguments before they were made. In
clearly defining his position by stating that it was the abuse
and not the right use of the arts that he was attacking, he
removed most causes of difference between himself and his
opponents. Lodge freely admitted, "I abhore those poets that
savor of ribaldry, I will with the zealous admit the expullcion
of suche enormities;" and, "as I like Musik so admit I not
thos that deprave the same your Pipers are as odius to mee as
your self" (sigs. B2^V, B8). The only cause of contention
remaining between them was whether plays could be reformed
enough to make it allowable to act them. Lodge declared that
it was possible, Gosson that it was not.

iii

The Schoole of Abuse provoked replies from the players,
and probably also inspired others to attack the theaters in
turn. At least in the months following the appearance of
Gosson's first pamphlets, condemnations of the stage appeared
frequently. In November, 1579, shortly after the publication
of the Apologie, T. F.'s Newes from the North referred to the

Theater and Curtain as places of "expence" where time is "shame-
fully mispent" (sigs. L, F4). In the following year, 1580, the
opponents of the stage were especially active. In February
John Rainolds, Gosson's former teacher, published his Sex Theses
de Sacra Scriptura, et Ecclesia, in the preface to which he
called upon the people to destroy "the plagues of stageplayers,
the sights and shewes of Theaters."15 The following month
Thomas Lupton, in Siuqila, regretted that people should attend
plays and there "spend the time vaynely, and consume their
money fondely" (p. 27). Probably this year also F. Clement
added a passage to his Petie Schole in which he said:

> I have yet further to warne thee of an other...monstre
> horrible to beholde, I meane common playes which do no
> lesse, yea rather more metamorphize, transfigure, deforme,
> pervert and alter the harts of their haunters. But sith
> their chiefest Stages (of good men thought fit standerdes
> to display the streemes of the divels flags) labour now
> with such discredit, that al the honest abhorre them, doe
> thou also bid them...to leape the ladder, with this
> antiphony or countersonge advising better the Histrions:
> > Vile Theatron eat pessum Cortina labascat:
> > Scenica nunc Comus cesset adulteria.
> > Let vile Theater wag to wracke,
> > And Courtaine couch streightwayes:
> > Let Comus, cob of all misrule,
> > Now ceese adulterous playes.16

Even the elements conspired against the players. On April
6 there was a slight earthquake in London and adjoining regions.
Some dozen pamphlets and broadsides discussing it appeared almost immediately, most of which explained that the tremors were
a punishment sent by God because of the Londoners' sins. Antnon

---

15. Translated at the end of The Summe of the Conference
(1584), sig. Xx2^v.

16. The Petie Schole with an English Orthographie (1587),
p. 40. The only two extant copies of this work were printed
in 1587, though it was entered on the Stationers' Register in
1580, and the preface is dated 1576. On p. 32 Clement says
that "a good pause after the publishing here of" he was asked
to set down "whatsoever els I should thinke convenient to be
taught in this Schoole," and so he added an essay on the
love of books, which contains the references to the drama
quoted above. The entry in the Stationers' Register probably
indicates that the revision was made in 1580. I am indebted
to Miss Kathrine Koller for calling Clement's remarks to my
attention.

Mundy, reporting the episode in his View of sundry Examples,
said that "at the play houses the people came running foorth
supprised with great astonishment" (sig. D4ᵛ). Abraham Fleming,
in his A Bright Burning Beacon, saw it as an "Alarum bell, to
all prophaners of Gods sacred Sabbaoth, and specially to players,
plaiemakers, and all such as favor that damnable facultie," and
said:

> Tremble and quake therefore O yee shameles breakers
> of Gods Sabbaoth, which display your banners of vanitie,
> selling wind for monie, infecting the tender mindes of
> youth with the poison of your prophanations, kindling in
> them the fire of inordinate lust, to the wounding both of
> bodie and soule. Doth not God see your filtnines, or
> thinke you that your trade of life depending wholy upon
> those your Heathenish exercises, are not offensive to his
> Majestie? Will he winke at such wickednes, and keepe
> silence at such filthines as is continually concluded
> upon and committed in your Theatre, Curtaine, and accursed
> courtes of spectacles? Oh how glorious a worke should
> that be... to see all such abhominable places dedicated
> to Gentilisme, or rather Atheisme...utterly torne up from
> the foundations. (sigs. D3ᵛ-4)

In addition, two ballads attacking the stage, entitled respect-
ively, Comme from the plaie and A Ringinge Retraite,[17] were
hawked about the streets. Those who said that the earthquake
was sent as a punishment for sin conveniently overlooked the
fact that the only fatalities resulting from it occurred in
Christ's Church, where a man and woman listening to the sermon
were killed by falling masonry.

The most significant attack of the year appeared in October,
entitled A second and third blast of retrait from plaies and
Theatres. The anonymous author, who was quite certainly
Anthony Mundy,[18] explained in his preface that the first blast
had been given by Gosson, that the second blast was a translation from Book VI of Bishop Salvian's De Gubernatione Dei, and
that the third blast was his own. He objected to plays "because they are publike enimies to virtue, and religion; allure-
ments unto sinne; corrupters of good manners; the cause of
securitie and carelesnes; meere brothel houses of Bauderie:
and bring both the Gospel into slander; the Sabboth into

---

17. These are not extant, and are known only from the
entries in the Stationers' Register (ed. Arber, II, 368, 381).
18. See J. Dover Wilson, "Anthony Munday, Pursuivant and
Pamphleteer," MLR, IV (1909), 484-7; and Celeste Turner Wright,
Anthony Mundy (Berkeley, 1928), Chapter V.

contempt; mens soules into danger; and finalie the whole Common-
weale into disorder" (ed. Hazlitt, p. 121). Mundy also was a
reformed playwright; but his reformation was only temporary because, as Gosson later remarked, he soon returned to his vomit
again.

Though the Third blast is a dull piece of writing, and
though much of it retraverses ground that had already been well
covered by Gosson, it is interesting on at least three counts.
First, it bore the city arms on the reverse of the title page,
and so seems to have been directly inspired by the London authorities. Second, considerable use is made of arguments based upon
Biblical authority. Mundy said that he had been a playwright
himself; but "when it pleased God of his mercie to cal mee to
the reading of his worde, and diligent studie of the Scriptures,
I began to loath my former life, and to mislike my owne doings"
(p. 124). His major argument against the theaters is that
attendance at them breaks the Third and Fourth Commandments,
which deal with blasphemy and keeping the Sabbath. Third, it
outlines a practical program of reform, by suggesting that Sunday performances be prohibited and that something be done about
reducing the patronage extended to players by the nobility. The
Third blast shows that a new phase of the controversy was beginning. Formerly, those who attacked the stage were willing
to admit that plays were commendable if properly used, and con-
tented themselves with pointing out the social inconveniences
caused by commercial performances. But Mundy asserted that the
drama was evil in principle, and was flatly prohibited by the
word of God.

Meanwhile, the players were not idle. Lodge's reply to
the Schoole of Abuse was probably printed late in 1579, but was
suppressed by the licensers--another indication of the interest
taken by the civic authorities in the controversy. Lodge's
tract was hastily put together and carelessly printed. It
attempted to answer, one by one, Gosson's charges in the Schoole
of Abuse, but relied as much upon personal invective as upon
argument. Most of its positive statements concerning plays
were translated bodily from the Praenotamenta, an introductory
sketch of the nature and history of classical drama, prepared
by the French printer Badius Ascensius in 1502 as a preface to
an edition of Terence.[19]

In addition to Lodge's reply, a scene was interpolated
in R. W.'s play, The Three Ladies of London, in which the

---

19. See my article, "The Source of Lodge's Reply to
Gosson," RES, XV (1939), 364-71.

didactic value of comedies was demonstrated.[20] Later, on February 23, 1582, the Playe of playes was acted at the Theater. The purpose of this morality was to show that recreation is necessary to life and that plays, if their "matter be purged, deformities blazed, sinne rebuked, honest mirth intermingled, and fitte time for the hearing of the same appointed," are pleasant and necessary in a commonwealth.[21] The actors, in other words, admitted the justice of some of the charges against them, and at least expressed a willingness to attempt reform. But by this time reform was not enough to satisfy the opponents of the theaters; nothing less than extirpation would do. At first objection had been made only to the social evils caused by commercial performances; but now the very principle of dramatic presentations was called in question and was asserted to be evil. Gosson had popularized the first phase of the attack, and he likewise was a leader of the second.

Gosson had borne the brunt of the players' counter-attack. He had been called an ass in Straunge newes and had been sneered at by Lodge as an ignoramus, a hypocrite, and a beggar. Smarting under the indignities to which he had been subjected, he returned to the controversy and on April 6, 1582, the second anniversary of the London earthquake, entered for publication Playes Confuted in five Actions, Proving that they are not to be suffred in a Christian common weale, by the waye both the Cavils of Thomas Lodge, and the Play of Playes.

He gave over his ornate Euphuistic style and wrote plainly and sternly. He went beyond the social abuses of theaters and stigmatized as sinful the element of fiction--or, as he chose to call it, counterfeiting--in performances. He did not depend upon authority or ancient examples to prove his points, but grounded his arguments philosophically and gave them logical development. Playes Confuted is the most carefully considered and acutely argued essay against the drama produced by any Elizabethan or Jacobean critic. Even William Prynne, with his monumental catalogue of over 260 authors who disapproved of plays, heathen and christian, foreign and domestic, was unable to add any significant arguments.

Gosson divided his work into five actions proportionable to the five acts of a play, each of the first four acts deal-

---

20. This scene is not in the printed text of the play (1584), but is outlined by Gosson in Playes Confuted, sigs. D-D2, p. 185.

21. The play is not extant, but Gosson refers to a performance of it in Playes Confuted, sig. D5, p. 189; and gives an outline of the plot, sigs. Fv-F2, pp. 201-2.

ing with the drama under the heading of one of the Aristotelian
"causes." In the first action he dealt with the efficient
cause of plays, that is, discussed their origin. They are not
to be permitted in a Christian commonwealth, he said, because
they are "the doctrine and invention of the Devill" and are ,
"consecrated to idolatrie." (sig. B4^V, p. 171). He illustrated
his argument with the quotation of many Biblical texts and of
works by Ambrose, Augustine, and Tertullian.

In the second action he discussed the material cause of
plays, what they were made of; and here he replied directly to
Lodge's assertion, made on the alleged authority of Cicero,
that a play is "the Schoolmistresse of life; the lookinge
glasse of manners; and the image of trueth."[22] How can plays
teach, he asked, when tragedies treat of nothing but cruelty and
murder, comedies of nothing but wanton love and cosenage? "The
best play you can picke out, is but a mixture of good and evill,
how can it be then the schoolemistres of life?" (sig. C5^V, p.
180). Milton's attack on "fugitive and cloistered virtue" provided the answer to Gosson's question; but that was not made
until more than sixty years later.

Neither can a play, said Gosson, in which corruption of
manners is revealed, be a "Glasse of behaviour." A judge, or
one who reprehends the faults of others, ought to be grave
and uncorrupted; but players are flighty men who lead wanton
lives and who write, not for the advancement of virtue, but
out of a spirit of malice or vainglory. Lastly, a play cannot be an image of truth, because either "those thinges are
fained that never were"--the story of Cupid and Psyche, for
example--or the playwrights pervert true histories by changing
the order of events, interpolating inauthentic episodes, and
making the action longer or shorter than it really was (sig.
D4-4^V, p. 188). This is similar to Plato's charge that poets
distort reality, because they are merely imitators of imitations,
at a third remove from truth.

In the third action he dealt with the formal cause of
plays, the manner of their presentation by actors before an

---

22. Fol. C4, p. 179; from Lodge's Reply, fol. C2^V. Actually Lodge was quoting Badius Ascensius, who was quoting Dona-
tus' Commentum de Comoedia (v, 1): "Comoediam esse, Cicero ait,
imitationem vitae, speculum consuetudinis, imaginem veritatis."
The statement, as Gosson pointed out, is not found in Cicero's
extant writings. The definition was highly esteemed and frequently referred to in the sixteenth century--see Schoole of
Abuse, fol. B5, p. 31; Sidney, Defence of Poesie (1595), fol.
E4^V; Shakespeare, Hamlet, III, II, 23-8.

audience. To play is to lie, and to lie is to sin, Gosson argued. Furthermore, women's parts were taken by men or boys, and "the Law of God very straightly forbids men to put on womens garments;" yet players put on "not the apparell onely, but the gate, the gestures, the voyce, the passions of a woman." They therefore "falsifie, forge and adulterate," and are "abomination unto the Lord." (sig. E3, p. 195). The proof text for this statement is Deuteronomy xxii:5--

> A woman shall not wear that which pertaineth unto a man, neither shall a man put on a woman's garment: for whosoever doeth these things is an abomination unto the Lord thy God.

This became the most effective argument used by the Elizabethans against the theater, because it had definite Biblical authority behind it. John Rainolds made it the basis of his Overthrow of Stage-Playes, and most opponents of the stage after Gosson's time used it. William Crashaw, the father of the poet, was so convinced by it that he preached two sermons, one in 1608 and another in 1610, against actors, and it was not until John Selden explained the text to him as applying to the ceremonial rather than to the moral law that he gave over his attack. Alberico Gentili, the leading professor of civil law in England, took the question under consideration, and Prynne used it as a mainstay in his Histrio-Mastix.[23]

Yet Gosson was not satisfied with the authority of the Bible alone, and grounded his argument on further philosophical considerations. He consulted the works of Aristotle and St. Thomas Aquinas for the definition of a lie and a discussion of the evils of lying, and by this means he was able to prove that acting was a species of counterfeiting and so was sinful. (sig. E4-4ᵛ, pp. 196-7). Shakespeare, who was well read in anti-stage literature, a few years later played with this further argument, turned it around, and produced from it one of his great comic scenes--Falstaff's famous soliloquy on counter-

---

23. Gosson was not the originator of the argument. It had been used centuries earlier by the Church Fathers, and had been revived by Calvin in a sermon preached in 1556 (Chambers, Eliz. Stage, I, 248). Northbrooke noted that "Saint Cyprian vehemently inveygheth againste those which, contrarie to nature and the lawe, doe attire themselves, being men, in women's apparell" (Treatise, ed. Collier, p. 101); but he made no further use of the statement and apparently did not regard it as important. Gosson was the first Englishman to develop its full implications and to bring it forcibly to the attention of his contemporaries.

feiting:

> Counterfeit? I lie, I am no counterfeit: to die,
> is to be a counterfeit; for he is but the counterfeit of
> a man who hath not the life of a man: but to counterfeit
> dying, when a man thereby liveth, is to be no counter-
> feit, but the true and perfect image of life indeed.
> (Henry IV, Part One, V, iv, 116 ff.)

As Gosson explained, "For a meane person to take upon him the
title of a Prince with counterfeit porte, and traine, is by
outwarde signes to shewe them selves otherwise then they are,
and so with in the compasse of a lye, which by Aristotles
judgement is naught of it selfe and to be fledde" (sig. E4ᵛ,
p. 197).

At this point Gosson replied to the argument that learned
and godly men, like Gregory Nazianzen and George Buchanan, had
written plays. His refutation of this was that they had
written not plays, but dialogues like those of Plato and
Cicero. He was willing to admit that it was proper to read
plays, if their matter were honest; but asserted that it was
sinful to act them. Rainolds, when in 1592 he engaged in
controversy with William Gager over the lawfulness of academic
drama, took the same position. "But it is one thing to recite;
an other thing to play," he said, and referred to Juvenal,
Pliny, and Scaliger, "who dispraised not Poets for reciting
comedies, yet thought a man ought rather choose to dye then
play them."[24] Rainolds's whole line of argument corresponds
so closely with the argument of Playes Confuted, that one
wonders whether he had helped Gosson in any way. He was in
London during the summer and autumn of 1580 and frequently
thereafter, so that Gosson could easily have consulted him
at the time he wrote his last pamphlet against the stage.

In the fourth action Gosson dealt with the final cause
of plays, which he said was "to make our affections overflow"
(sig. Fᵛ, p. 201). This was designed as a direct reply to
the Play of Playes, which had accused him of immoderate zeal
and had argued that delight is necessary to life and that
comedies are a means of honest recreation which give delight.
He countered this argument by praising the virtue of temperance,
from which he deduced that, as comedies breed excess of laughter
and tragedies excess of weeping, both are enemies to temperance.
He also drew a distinction between carnal and spiritual delight, the former of which we should hold in check, while we
should encourage the latter. We should not rejoice in the
world, but in God; we should live not for ourselves, but

24. Th' Overthrow of Stage-Plays, p. 22.

for Christ. In the fifth action he dealt with the effects of
plays, which he said "effeminate and soften the hearts of men"
and lead them to vice. This section reaffirms arguments that
had previously been brought forward in the Schoole of Abuse.
    The new line of argument used by Mundy in the Third blast
and by Gosson in Playes Confuted had an immediate effect upon
the anti-stage controversy. In 1583 Philip Stubbes published
his Anatomie of Abuses, which contained a section entitled
"Of Stage-playes and Enterluds, with their wickednes." A
considerable part of this was made up of extracts from Playes
Confuted. The same year Gervase Babington published his Very
Fruitful Exposition of the Commandements, which went through
many later editions. In this work Babington pointed out that
to attend plays was a manifest breach of the Seventh Command-
ment (1596 ed., pp. 137, 158). Later commentators, such as
Dod and Cleaver in their Plaine and familiar Exposition of the
Ten Commaundements (1604), did the same (1606 ed., p. 294).
This theological phase of the controversy exerted considerable
influence upon public opinion, and was an important factor in
bringing about the eventual closing of the theaters in 1642.
    The Gosson-Lodge debate came to an end in 1584, when Lodge,
in an epistle to the gentlemen of the Inns of Court before his
Alarum against Usurers, withdrew as gracefully as he could
from the controversy. He admitted that defending plays was a
slight subject, and made no attempt to uphold the position he
had earlier taken. The general tenor of the epistle shows
that by this time he had gone over to his opponent's camp at
least to the extent of no longer considering plays worth defending. His only objection was to the aspersions Gosson had
cast on his personal character: "If thy cause wer good, I
doubt not but in so large and ample a discourse as thou hadst
to handle, thou mightest had left the honor of a gentleman
inviolate" (sig. A4).
    But though the principals in the earlier years of the
controversy had withdrawn from active participation, the
attack itself continued, sometimes with more and sometimes with
less violence. By 1584 it had reached such proportions, and
had aroused so much public interest, that the authorities at
Oxford proposed as one of the subjects of the disputations for
the M.A. degree in that year the question, "Utrum ludi scenici
in bene instituta civitate probandi sint?"[25]
    Up to this point very little has been said of the activities
of the civic authorities in suppressing plays. It was pointed

---

    25. Andrew Clark, Register of the University of Oxford
(Oxford, 1887), II, i, 171.

out earlier that up to 1577 their activities had been merely
regulatory, not repressive, and that the licensing act of 1574,
had been designed mainly to protect the audiences that attended
performances. During the years 1577-1579, when the pamphleteering phase of the controversy was rapidly gaining momentum,
the Mayor and Aldermen remained, on the surface, inactive. The
only record we have from this period of legislation designed to
control the theaters, is a permanent order issued by the Privy
Council in March, 1579, prohibiting plays during Lent.

But this apparent inactivity does not necessarily prove
that the London officials held aloof from the controversy.
Though the Mayor and Aldermen had authority within the city itself, they could not effectively combat the players without
the aid of the Queen's Privy Council, because the theaters
were outside the city limits and so did not come within the
city's jurisdiction, and because the royal government could
circumvent the city ordinances by issuing special patents to
companies of actors, or by bringing pressure upon the city
authorities to give permission for playing. The only way the
Mayor and Aldermen could effectively implement their legislation
was to gain the assistance of the royal government, and the
only way they could gain this assistance was to prove that
the conditions they wished to remedy were dangerous and that
public opinion desired their remedy. The best way, therefore,
to control the theaters was to arouse public opinion against
them.

In an earlier chapter I have given reasons for believing
that the London authorities, or at least some group of city
merchants, actively furthered the attack on the stage that
was carried on from the pulpit and press. Most of the attacks
by clergymen were delivered from Paul's Cross, appointment to
which was under official control. The city arms on the reverse
of the title page of the Second and third blast shows that
the Corporation at least approved of its arguments, and Mundy's
profession as a hack writer makes it unlikely that he undertook its composition without remuneration. Likewise, the
double printing of the first edition of Gosson's Schoole of
Abuse shows that the publication of that tract was something
more than the independent business venture of a single book-
seller.

The pamphleteers attacked the theaters because they gave
occasion for immoral acts, because attending them on Sundays
kept people from church, and because they were a waste of time
and money. The objection to Sunday performances, which many
who otherwise defended players upheld, was finally met in
December, 1581, by a letter from the Privy Council permitting
plays on week days only.[26] But this made all the more serious

the objection that attending plays was a waste of time and
money. The Theater and Curtain had no provision for illuminating their stages, so performances were of necessity given
during the daylight hours, usually at between three and five
in the afternoon. For a London artisan or his apprentice to
attend the theater, therefore, meant that he had to take a
full half-day off from work. It was this situation that
especially disturbed the industrious merchants and master craftsmen. It would disturb our business executives and manufacturers
today, if their employees regularly absented themselves from
their jobs one or two afternoons a week in order to go to the
moving pictures. It cannot be denied that Londoners had a
legitimate cause of grievance against the theaters.

However, the city authorities took no direct hand in the
controversy until the campaign from press and pulpit had been
carried on for about two years, at which time public opinion
had been considerably aroused. Then, in 1580, they began
trying to enlist the support of the Privy Council. On April
12 the Lord Mayor wrote to the Lord Chancellor, pointed out
that commercial dramatic performances corrupted the youth of
the city, gave occasion for disorders, and endangered public
health in time of plague, and asked that "the said playes and
toumbelers be wholy stayed and forbidden as ungodlye and peril-
ous, as well at those places nere our liberties as within the
jurisdiction of this Cittie." Nothing came of this request,
however, and the civic authorities had to find their own means
of getting rid of the disorders. In November, 1581, the Lord
Mayor issued an order forbidding the posting of play bills;
and in April, 1582, he issued another order requiring all
freemen of the livery companies, under pain of punishment,
to forbid their apprentices from going to any plays either
within or without the city. The posting of play bills had
earlier been objected to by Stockwood, and the restraint of
apprentices had been suggested by Gosson in his Apologie.

Finally, Article 62 of Orders Appointed to be Executed
in the Cittie of London, probably issued sometime in 1582,
provided that all "Enterludes in publique places, and the
resort to the same shall wholy be prohibited as ungodly, and
humble sute be made to the Lords that lyke prohibition be in
places neere unto the Cittie." This was the first attempt on
the part of the Mayor and Aldermen to abolish commercial performances entirely. However, difficulties were met in trying
to enforce this order, as is shown by a series of documents

26. This and the following documents referred to are
printed by Chambers, Eliz. Stage, IV, 284 ff.

among the Lansdowne Manuscripts dating from 1584 or 1585, which
include a petition from the players and an elaborate reply from
the Corporation of London addressed to the Privy Council.[27]
For many years the city was worsted in the encounter, and though
the Mayor and Aldermen were able to hinder playing, they were
not able to suppress it. The royal government supported the
actors, and without its assistance the London authorities could
not institute effective action. But one thing the controversy
did accomplish; that was to arouse public opinion, so that more
and more prominent citizens became convinced that the commercialized stage should be controlled or even abolished.

iv

It is unfortunate that scholars have labelled this early
attack on the stage "the Puritan attack," for such a label
obscures some of the fundamental issues involved. The preceding survey has shown that Gosson took a prominent and leading
part in the early phases of the controversy, and yet instead
of being a Puritan, he was acutally a vigorous opponent of
Puritanism. If a similarly minute biographical investigation
were made of the other persons involved, it may very well
appear that several of them were likewise opposed to Puritanism.
Efficient government and sound morality is not the monopoly of
any particular party or sect. Anglican divines were just as
much disturbed over the evils of playgoing and just as outspoken in their opinions as the most rabid Puritans. The
early attack on the stage was not brought about by external
forces, such as the rise to prominence of the Puritans; but
was caused by the development of certain objectionable conditions, resulting from the commercialization of the drama, within the theaters themselves. Furthermore, early hostility to
the theaters was motivated quite as much by political, economic,
and sanitary considerations as it was by religious and moral
prejudices.

We may summarize the events of the controversy from 1558
to 1585 as follows: (1) There is no evidence of any appreciable
prejudice against the drama or acting in England until the
year 1577. (2) By 1577 the theatrical business, formerly of
insignificant proportions, had become a considerable industry
as a result of the building of the Theater and Curtain outside
London. The city authorities objected to these new theaters
because they endangered public health, public order, and public
decency; and they were seconded by certain members of the

---

27. Printed in the Malone Society <u>Collections</u>, I, 169-79.

clergy, whose aid they may have directly enlisted, who objected
to the stage because players enticed congregations from the
churches on Sundays and gave performances that were harmful to
public morals. The merchants and master craftsmen of the city
objected to plays, because they kept their apprentices from
work and encouraged them to spend money which they could not
afford. These were the arguments advanced against the stage
until about the year 1580. Obviously it would be more appropriate to call this a "middle-class" attack than a "Puritan"
attack. It was not so much the clergy as it was the sober and
practical merchant folk who disapproved of elaborate professional dramatic entertainments. They were industrious and frugal
people who were annoyed by the disorder, idleness, waste, and
frivolity caused by the theaters. On the other hand, they did
not at first object to plays and acting in themselves, but only
to the abuses for which the theaters were responsible.

(3) The second phase of the attack was begun by Mundy's
Second and Third Blast, and firmly established by Gosson's
Playes Confuted. In this phase not only were the abuses of
plays and theaters criticized, but acting by its very nature
was declared to be sinful and contrary to the laws of God and
man. From this time forward the controversy took a theological
turn. The playhouses were still attacked because of the social
evils they caused, and in addition they were proved unlawful
by quotations from the Bible. The legislators likewise shifted
their ground. In 1574 the Common Council had been satisfied
to prescribe laws for the proper supervision of commercial performances, and issued orders which showed "how plaies were to
be tollerated and used." But the evils increased rather than
diminished, so that by 1582 they were led to issue orders
which required that plays "shall wholy be prohibited." Both
the civic authorities and the pamphleteers began with a willingness to tolerate certain plays, and ended by demanding their
absolute suppression.

To demand that the public theaters should be suppressed
was to take the most direct, but not the most effective way
of solving the problem. Milton saw the difficulty plainly
when, in Areopagitica, he said: "They are not skilful con-
siderers of human things, who imagine to remove sin by removing
the matter of sin...Banish all objects of lust, shut up all
youth into the severest discipline that can be exercised in
any hermitage, ye cannot make them chaste, that came not
thither so." For a long time better judgments prevailed, the
royal government tolerated and even encouraged plays, and
Shakespeare and his fellows were allowed to write and perform.
But the Long Parliament was not so tolerant, and on September
2, 1642, it passed an ordinance which decreed that all

"public stage-plays shall cease and be forborne." Thereafter, for more than two decades, England was deprived of legitimate dramatic entertainment.

CHAPTER V: STYLE AND STRUCTURE

i

If Gosson angered some of his contemporaries by his arguments, he pleased almost all of them with his style. The popularity of the Schoole of Abuse, the Ephemerides of Phialo and the Apologie of the Schoole of Abuse was to a great extent the result of the lively, witty, and ornate manner in which they were written. Indeed, the Schoole of Abuse and the Apologie stand almost alone among the scores of Elizabethan and Jacobean attacks on the stage as pamphlets which even today can still be read with some degree of pleasure; and the Ephemerides is the equal, at least so far as phrasing is concerned, of Lyly's far more famous Euphues. Even Gosson's enemy, Lodge, admitted in his Alarum against Usurers: "Now in publike I confesse thou hast a good pen, and if thou keepe thy Methode in discourse, and leave thy slandering without cause, there is no doubt but thou shalt bee commended for thy coppie, and praised for thy stile" (fol. A4ᵛ).

To write a praiseworthy style was clearly part of Gosson's intention, for he proclaimed it as his object in the Latin motto from Cicero that he put on the title page of the Schoole of Abuse: "To commit your thoughts to writing without being able to arrange or express them clearly or to attract the reader by some sort of pleasure, is the mark of a man who makes an extravagant misuse of both his leisure and his pen." His education had well equipped him to arrange his arguments effectively and to express them in a pleasing manner. He closed the "Epistle Dedicatorie" to his Ephemerides by requesting Master Philip Sidney "to vouchsafe them the reading, bicause you are learned; and to yelde them your patronage, sith they carie some taste of the Universitie." As Sidney had been a student at Oxford himself, he hardly needed this specific statement to remind him that Gosson's prose bore obvious traces of the college lecture room, and that his essays were composed on the model of the disputations held in the university schools.

In the sixteenth century an Oxford student heard lectures and listened to the disputations in the schools for his first two years of residence, and thereafter took part in the disputations himself at least once a term until he received his

degree. These exercises lasted two hours and were performed
by three persons at a time. One student, designated the re-
spondent, read a carefully prepared oration on an assigned
topic, and the other two students, designated opponents, answered him in turn; then the moderator in charge summed up
their arguments and gave judgment on their individual performances.[1] In preparing for these public disputations the undergraduates made a careful study of the textbooks on logic and
rhetoric; and when they wrote out their speeches, they constructed them according to the rules of the classical rhetoricians and the example of the Greek and Roman orators.

The text books usually divided orations into seven parts:
exordium, narratio, propositio, parititio, confirmatio, repre-
hensio, and peroratio--introduction, statement of the circumstances, statement of the point at issue, division of the
causes, arguments in support of the position, refutation of
the opposing arguments, and conclusion.[2] The preparation of
disputations was the most important exercise in literary composition performed by university students, and it is not surprising that, when they later wrote for other purposes, they
should use the same methods. Most prose treatises of Elizabeth's reign that pretended to any elegance were constructed
on this model. Sidney's Defence of Poesie, for example, con-
forms in all respects to the ideal pattern of the classical
oration, complete with the traditional seven parts.[3] Analysis
reveals a similar structure underlying Gosson's Schoole of
Abuse and Apologie, though neither of these works is so skil-
fully put together or so completely unified as Sidney's essay.

The unity of the Schoole of Abuse is partly disrupted because it is "a plesaunt invective against Poets, Pipers, Plaiers, Jesters, and such like Caterpillers of a Commonwelth,"
that is, it deals with some half dozen different subjects.
First, there come in order three separate orations devoted re-
spectively to poets, pipers, and players, with a peroration
common to all three; then, by way of digression, there is a
discussion of the abuses of dancers, tumblers, dicers, carders
fencers, and scholars; and, finally, there is a general conclusion. None of the sections of this work contains all seven

---

1. For a detailed description of these exercises, see
Andrew Clark, Register of the University of Oxford, II, Part
(Oxford, 1887), 21-66.
2. Thomas Wilson, Arte of Rhetorique, ed. G. H. Mair
(Oxford, 1909), p. 7.
3. See K. O. Myrick, Sir Philip Sidney as a Literary
Craftsman (Cambridge, U. S., 1935), pp. 46-83.

of the traditional divisions; but that was not required even by
the rhetoricians themselves. Cicero only lists five divisions.
     The argument against poetry in the first part of the
Schoole of Abuse begins with an exordium, an anecdote concerning the Syracusans. Then follows the narratio, or statement of
facts, in which it is said that poets always draw the worst hu-
mors to themselves and mix the bad with the good. Next comes
the propositio, a pithy sentence to sum up the whole matter,
which Gosson said he drew out of Cicero, to the effect that
poets are "the fathers of lyes, Pipes of vanitie, and Schooles
of Abuse." After this there is the partitio, or statement of
the arguments of the opponents which are to determine the topics of the discourse, and here Gosson uses Maximus Tyrius as
the straw man. Then follows the confirmatio, or proof, in
which detailed arguments, backed with copious historical examples, are advanced both to disprove the arguments of the opponents and to support the position taken. At this point there
properly should be a peroration to bring the discussion to a
close; but instead Gosson inserted a transitional paragraph
which introduces the subject of music. This section contains
only a propositio, and confirmatio; the peroratio does not come
until after the discussion of the third abuse, playing. Analysis reveals a similar structure ordering the arguments of the
Apologie.
     At first sight the Ephemerides appears to be different in
kind from the two works just discussed, because it ostensibly
tells a story and so ought to be considered as narrative rather
than as argument. Gosson explained his title by saying, "The
Daiesworks of Phialo, which spendeth his time in profitable
disputation among his freendes, I have called his Ephemerides,
after the maner of the Greekes" (fol. *4-4^V). As has been
mentioned before, the story was no more than a crude framework serving to hold together and introduce these profitable
disputations; the speeches were the real substance of the book,
and these were built upon the traditional pattern. Phialo's
first dissertation, which is typical of the rest, has as its
subject "A method which he ought to follow that desireth to
rebuke his freend." With its introduction, its statement of
the point at issue, its careful ordering of arguments and
examples under seven heads, and its conclusion, it follows
the form of the academic oration.
     Not only the form, but even the manner of presenting
academic orations was imitated in the Ephemerides. This is
most evident in the third part, titled "The defence of the
Curtezan, and her overthrowe." Philotimo speaks in praise of
Polyphile (fols. G6^V-H), Polyphile speaks in her own justification (fols. H-H5^V), Phialo confutes them both (fols. H5^V-

K6^V), and Jeraldi sums up the arguments and awards the victory to Phialo. This is precisely the manner of disputation in the university schools, for Philotimo and Polyphile perform as respondents, Phialo as opponent, and Jeraldi as moderator. The frequency with which this respondent-opponent-moderator device is used in other prose tales shows that the academic oration had considerable influence on the structure of Elizabethan works of fiction.[4]

It has been said that Gosson's Playes Confuted "has no intelligible arrangement of topics;"[5] but even a cursory reading shows that, just as the Schoole of Abuse and the Ephemerides derive their structure from the rhetorical exercises in the University, so Playes Confuted gets its principle of arrangement from the logical exercises. Gosson tells us himself at the beginning of his work that he will give us "a tast both of the causes of Plaies, and of the effectes" (fol. B3^V, p. 170); and near the end he says, "Therfore as I have already discovered the corruption of playes by the corruption of their causes, The Efficient, the Matter, the Forme, the end, so will I conclude the effects that this poyson works among us" (fol. G4, p. 213). In other words, the arguments in the "five Actions" of Playes Confuted, a division conformable to the five

---

4. Euphues's speech at the house of Lucilla on the question, "whether the qualities of the mynde, or the composition of the man, cause women most to lyke" (John Lyly, Works, ed. R. W. Bond [Oxford, 1902], I, 201-3), illustrates in form as well as in subject the academic oration. The meeting at Lady Flavia's house (ibid., II, 163-83), where three pairs of contestants dispute on three separate topics and Euphues acts as umpire to sum up and pass judgment, is a good example of the university disputation. Even closer to student practice is an episode in Brian Melbancke's Philotimus where the tutor of the two young men, Philotimus and Aemilius, "seing their could cheare...assignd them a question to dispute, to drive away the time. The question was this, whether it were better to take paines in youthe afterward to enjoye pleasure, or firste to revell him in the leaze of libertye, and in Age bee pinchte for his former sinnes" (1583, fol. H3). The ensuing debate occupies several pages. Formal disputations and orations were an integral part of the social life of the time. The pages of Holinshed show how important a part they played at official functions, especially during the visits of men of prominence to the universities.

5. Dover Wilson, in the Cambridge History of English Literature, VI (New York, 1910), 442.

acts of a play, are arranged in order under the headings of the four Aristotelian causes with a fifth section on effects. The first action is concerned with the efficient cause of plays, which Gosson says is the devil; the second with the material cause, which is a falsified representation of reality; the third with the formal cause, which is performance before an audience by players; the fourth with the final cause, which is the immoderate stirring of emotions; and the fifth with the effects, which are immoral conduct and sin.[6]

Gosson's last published work, his sermon the Trumpet of Warre, is also traditional in structure. The method of composing a sermon in the sixteenth-century was to choose a text-- in this case, II Chronicles, xx:20--to divide it into sections, and then to expound it at length phrase by phrase.[7] Gosson made two divisions, and used the first as a justification for a war against Spain and the second as a description of the rewards for a war undertaken in a just cause. In developing these two divisions he again put into practice the principles of structure he had learned while a student, since, as his teacher Rainolds had explained, the arts of logic and rhetoric "are requisit to preaching the woord," because by means of them ministers "learne the way of cutting it aright and applying it."[8]

ii

The aspect of Gosson's writings discussed in the preceding pages the rhetoricians of classical and Renaissance times called dispositio, "the which is nothing els but an apt bestowing, and orderly placing of things, declaring where every argument shall be set, and in what maner every reason shal be applied for confirmation of the purpose." An equally important division of rhetoric was elocutio, the "applying of apt

---

6. The arrangement of topics under the four Aristotelian causes was a favorite structural device with sixteenth-century preachers and controversialists. For examples, see Peter Martyr, Loci Communes (1576), p. 240; and John Rainolds, Oratio in Laudem Artis Poeticae (ed. Ringler and Allen, Princeton, 1940), p. 11.

7. For the structure of sixteenth-century sermons, see W. F. Mitchell, English Pulpit Oratory from Andrewes to Tillotson (1932), pp. 63 ff. and 99 ff.

8. Th' Overthrow of Stage-Playes ([Middleburg], 1599), p. 125.

wordes and sentences to the matter."9 Dispositio we call
structure, elocutio, style. It was in this second department
of rhetorical exercise that Gosson excelled, and he became
especially popular with his contemporaries because he wrote
the "new English" that was given the name of Euphuism.

Euphuism takes its name from John Lyly's Euphues, which
was published in December, 1578. Though Lyly was the most
influential, Gosson takes at least second place in that small
group of writers who, about the year 1579, were responsible
for introducing the new style into English. They were followed by such men as Austin Saker, Anthony Mundy, Brian Melbancke,
William Averell, John Dickenson, and many others, notably
Lodge and Greene, so that for the next few years Euphuism was
the prevailing literary language, the accepted mode for dedications, novels, and other works that were thought to require
an ornate and stately prose. The important position in the
history of Elizabethan prose held by this new manner of writing, which Gosson was influential in popularizing, makes some
discussion of it desirable.

Euphuism has been called "the least elusive of styles,
being deliberately compounded and, therefore, easily analysed;"
but the various meanings that have been given the term, even
by modern scholars, show that there has been a considerable
difference of opinion concerning its analysis. Sir Walter
Scott thought that it was similar to the periphrastical style
that "predominates in the romances of Calprenede and Scuderi;"
George Eliot and Dickens, who should have known better, used
the term as a synonym for euphemism; and even as accomplished
a scholar as J. E. Spingarn equated it with the "metaphysical"
sermon style of the early seventeenth century. In analysing
it, present day scholars have emphasized sometimes its use of
antithesis, sometimes its schematic structure, and sometimes
its far fetched similes and illustrations. What needs to be
emphasized is that Euphuism is characterized, not by any
single stylistic device, but by a peculiar combination of
several such devices.

Though the moderns have been uncertain about its definition, the Elizabethans had no doubts about it whatever. They
were quick to notice and to comment on the peculiarities of
the new prose, and John Hoskins in particular gave a fairly
complete and adequate description of its more important
characteristics. Discussing the rhetorical figure paronomasia,

---

9. Wilson, Rhetorique, p. 6.
10. J. W. H. Atkins in the Cambridge History of English
Literature, III (New York, 1909), 394.

which he defined as "a pleasant touch of the same letter, syl-
lable, or word, with a different meaning," he said:

> Lyly, the author of Euphues, seeing the dotage
> of the time upon this small ornament, invented varie-
> ties of it; for he disposed the agnominations [i.e.,
> alliterations] in as many fashions as repetitions
> are distinguished...sometimes the first word and the
> middle harped one upon another, sometimes the first
> and the last...and this with a measure, compar--a
> change of contention, or contraries--and a device
> of a similitude, in those days made a gallant show.

Later he defined parison as:

> An even gait of sentences answering each other
> in measures interchangeably, such as in St. Augustine
> but often in Gregory the Divine [i.e., Nazianzen],
> such as in the Bishop of W. [i.e., Bilson] his books
> which he hath written in English, and many places of
> Euphues; but that St. Austin, Bilson, and Lyly do
> very much mingle this figure with agnominatio and
> similiter cadens. It is a smooth and memorable style
> for utterance, but in the penning it must be used
> moderately and modestly.[11]

Gabriel Harvey especially singled out for comment Lyly and
Greene's "euphuing of Similes;"[12] and Nashe, who disliked the
character of the extraneous ornament of the new style--though
his own writings were not entirely free from the affectations he
criticized--expressed the hope that, if Euphuistic writers
would betake themselves to a new trade, "the Presse should be
farre better employed, histories of antiquitie not halfe so
much belyed; Minerals, stones, and herbes should not have such
cogged natures and names ascribed to them without cause."[13]
    The characteristics of Euphuism as contemporary critics
understood them may then be summarized as follows: First, it
is a declamatory prose style--"a smooth and memorable style
for utterance"--excessively ornate and especially suited for
courtly correspondence, polite fiction, and epideictic orations.
Second, it is characterized by the use of rhetorical figures

---

11. Directions for Speech and Style [c. 1599], ed. H. H.
Hudson (Princeton, 1935), pp. 16, 37.
    12. Works, ed. A. B. Grosart (n. p., 1884), II, 125.
    13. Works, ed. R. B. McKerrow (1910), I, 10.

known as schemes, that is, by the arrangement of words in a vocal or oral pattern. This is most often accomplished by setting parisonic members in schematic opposition and by ornamenting the individual clauses with alliteration and other forms of consonance--"a measure...a change of contention, or contraries" mingled with "agnominatio and similiter cadens." Third, this elaborately patterned prose is further heightened with incidental ornament in the form of historical allusions, similes, and proverbs--"a device of a similitude." These are seldom introduced singly, but are heaped together in the schematic form of cumulation (frequentatio). Fourth, these illustrative examples are exceptional in that they are often of a fabulous nature and are either drawn from recondite sources or are the pure products of the author's fancy.[14]

All of these devices may be found together on page after page of Gosson's early works. For example, in the Ephemerides he wrote:

> The feete of Thetis were as brighte as silver, but the ankles of Hebe, cleerer than Cristall; The armes of Aurora as ruddy as the Rose, but the brestes of Juno, as whyte as snowe; Minerva was wise, but Juno was welthie, and Venus in beautie stayned them both. Jewelles are all precious, but not all of one price, nor all of one vertue, nor of like perfection. The Adamant of nature draweth Iron, but the stone Hematites dooth stoppe blood. The Carbuncle in darknesse shineth like fire, but the Topase is holp with the light of the Sunne. Thus may you perceive, that all Rivers have not their course into one Sea, all fruite doth not grow upon one tree, all fishe, is not taken in one streame, all fashions, are not cut out of one cloth. (fols. C8^v-D)

In this passage the series of antithetical clauses, the elaborate schemes, the cumulated mythological allusions, and the learned comparisons and illustrations are so obvious that extended analysis is unnecessary.

The devices of Euphuism were not in themselves new, for they had been used, separately, by earlier Tudor writers. It

---

14. Lyly drew much of his "unnatural natural history" from Pliny and the compendiums of Erasmus; Gosson used Plutarch. Robert Greene was the most notorious offender in the invention of spurious examples--see D. C. Allen, "Science and Invention in Greene's Prose," PMLA, LIII (1938), 1007-18.

was the peculiar way in which these old devices were combined
that made the Elizabethans signify the individuality of the
style by giving it a name of its own. George Pettie's Petite
Pallace (1576) is highly schematic, but cumulated allusions
and similes from strange sources are rare. John Grange's
Golden Aphroditis (1577) contains many learned similes and
allusions heaped together, but the prose lacks a clearly defined schematic structure. Neither of these works is entirely
Euphuistic, because the distinguishing mark of the "new English"
is the combination of both schematic structure and learned ornament in paragraphs--the paragraph and not the sentence is the
unit of construction. The arrangement of the elements within
each paragraph is characterized by repetition, repetition of
the same schematic devices and of similar illustrative details.
Lyly's Euphues is the earliest work in English known to be
written in the fully developed Euphuistic style.

      The Schoole of Abuse, the Ephemerides, and the Apologie
are all Euphuistic, the Ephemerides more so than the rest; but
though this latter work was designed in part as a reply to the
Anatomy of Wyt, Gosson did not copy his style from Lyly. For
the model of his prose, as for the model of the structure of
his writings, we must look to Oxford. Between 1572 and 1578
John Rainolds was the Greek Reader of Corpus and regularly
lectured, in Latin, to the entire University three times a
week. According to the testimony of his contemporaries, he
soon became the most popular lecturer in the University. His
listeners were especially attracted by the style of his orations, which was apparently original with him, and which contains all the elements of the fully developed Euphuistic style.
For example, in a lecture he delivered at the beginning of the
Christmas term in 1574, in one short passage he heaped together
mythological allusions--to Sysiphus, Tityos, and the Belides
among others; used illustrations from natural history--the
chameleon that lives on air, Pliny's account of the overflow-
ing of the Nile, etc.; and twisted his prose into elaborate
schematic patterns. The following sentences are typical:

          Ita sunt nobis animi pestilentibus afflati
      morbis, ut insalubria quam salubria, id est, quae
      placent, quam quae prosunt, fucatae Philosophiae,
      quam syncerae sapientiae, delirantium Gentilium,
      quam prudentium Christianorum, caliginum et vitiorum
      et errorum, quam lucis et virtutis et veritatis ele-
      menta dicam, an venena potius percipere malimus.
      Quid est melle gustatu suavius? at hominibus affectis
      morbo Regio videtur mel amarum, felle vesci gratius.
      Ecquis carbones putat salubres? at a mulierculis

Pica laborantibus cretam et carbones, tanquam nectar
et ambrosiam, desyderari tradunt.[15]

This passage of completely Euphuistic prose was recited in
an Oxford lecture room several years before Lyly published his
Euphues. The proto-Euphuists Pettie and Grange, and the early
Euphuists Lyly, Gosson, and Lodge had all been students at
Oxford during the time that Rainolds was delivering his lectures.
Evidently each of them imitated the style from him, and later
introduced it into English.[16] It was from Rainolds, then, that
Gosson learned the devices of style that made his pamphlets so
attractive to his contemporaries.

iii

What Gosson really had to say in the Schoole of Abuse, the
Ephemerides, and the Apologie could have been effectively stat-
ed--effectively, that is, according to modern standards--in
about one-quarter the number of words he actually used. Con-
ciseness was not one of the virtues of the Euphuistic style;
but then it was not a quality especially admired by the Elizabethans. Their taste was formed upon criteria different from
ours and required a more bulky diet than that to which we are
accustomed. Although it took Gosson's Phialo some six printed pages merely to say that a man should not rebuke a friend
in adversity, Philotimo nevertheless marvelled at the "pithy-
nesse of his speech, which in al his conference never used a
waste worde" (fol. A8ᵛ).
    The characteristic of Gosson's prose especially commended
by Lodge was its "coppie." The word "copy"--the Latin "copia"
and the modern English "copiousness"--signified the amplifica-

---

15. "Oratio post Festum Natalis Christi, contra felici-
tatem Aristotelicam. 1574," printed in Rainolds's Orationes
Duodecim (1619), p. 201. The peculiar symptoms of those af-
flicted with the King's Evil are also referred to by Gosson in
the Apologie (L2ᵛ, p. 65); he probably derived his information
from Rainolds's lecture.
    16. The most authoritative discussion of the ultimate
origins of Euphuism is the essay by M. W. Croll, "The Sources
of the Euphuistic Rhetoric," prefacing Lyly's Euphues (1916),
pp. xv-lxiv. Additional material will be found in my introduction to Rainolds's Oratio in Laudem Artis Poeticae, pp. 12-15.
For a more elaborate discussion of Rainolds's part in origina-
ting and popularizing the style, see my article, "The Immediate
Source of Euphuism," PMLA, LIII (1938), 678-86.

tion of an argument or statement by elaborating it with many
words, many images, and many ideas. "Among all the figures of
Rhetorique," said Thomas Wilson, "there is no one that so much
helpeth forward an Oration, and beautifieth the same with such
delightful ornaments, as doth amplification" (p. 116). One
way of attaining this copiousness was by simple expansion. In
the Apologie, for example, Gosson extended Cicero's phrase,
"O tempora O mores," to: "O God, O men, O heaven, O earth,
O tymes, O manners, O miserable dayes" (fol. L8, p. 71). Ordinarily, however, he obtained this copiousness chiefly by
the use of historical anecdotes or illustrative examples, and
sententiae or proverbs.

It is a commonplace of rhetorical theory that "he that
mindeth to perswade, must needes be well stored with examples."
Therefore, Gosson made liberal use of both historical anecdotes
and illustrations from other sources, and he always applied
them effectively. An example of his use of the former can be
illustrated by reference to the opening passage of his Apologie.
His effective use of the latter is shown in the Schoole of
Abuse where, addressing the Lord Mayor of London, in place of
the bald statement that actors are very clever in evading the
law, he wrote instead:

> The fish Sepia can trouble the water to shun
> the nettes, that are shot to catch her: Torpedo
> hath craft inough at the first touch to inchant the
> hooke, to conjure the line, to bewitch the rod, and
> to benumme the handes of him that angleth. Whether
> our Players be the Spawnes of such fishes, I know
> not wel, yet I am sure that how many nets so ever
> ther be layde to take them, or hookes to choke them,
> they have Ynke in their bowels to darken the water,
> and sleights in their budgets, to dry up the arme of
> every Magistrate. (fols E7v-8, p. 56)

Proverbs and pithy sayings, which provided Gosson with his
third means for obtaining copiousness, he usually heaped together in clusters. Although this was recommended in the hand-
books on rhetoric, and though it had been done sparingly by a
few of his predecessors, its excessive use was peculiar to the
Euphuists. It was an unfortunate choice of ornament; some
passages in which it occurs often have no more literary quality,
and certainly less interest, than the pages of a dictionary.
But proverbs, which were looked upon as vulgar by the wits of
the Age of Anne and are considered trite today, were held in
high esteem by the Elizabethans and are found scattered over
the pages of writers as different in temperament as the school-

master Roger Ascham and the poet William Shakespeare.

Professor M. P. Tilley, who has made an exhaustive study
of the proverb lore in the works of Pettie and Lyly, found two
hundred and sixty-one different proverbs in the Petite Pallace
and six hundred and forty-three in Euphues.[17] Gosson went to
even greater lengths in using these bits of homely wisdom; in
the Schoole of Abuse, a work scarcely one-eighth as long as
the two parts of Lyly's Euphues, there are a hundred and eighty-
five proverbs and proverbial expressions. Most of these were
common and fairly well known--seventeen, for example, are
found in Heywood's Dialogue of Proverbs Concerning Marriage,
and thirty-three occur in the lists compiled by Professor
Tilley from Euphues and the Petite Pallace. Most of these
are popular in character as, "a rowling stone gathers no mosse,"
and "all the keys hang not at one mans girdle." Others, while
of literary origin, are part of the traditional stock, as the
phrase "draw Hercules shoes on a childs feet."

Sometimes Gosson's tags are popular quotations, as the
line from Mantuan, "semel insanivimus omnes," which every
schoolboy knew because it appeared in the grammar book. He
had even mastered the art of composing in proverbs, which he
did when he translated the line from Virgil, which he para-
phrased as "heu quod tam pingui macer est mihi taurus in arvo,"
with "alas here is fat feeding and leane beasts: or as one
said at the shearing of hogs, great cry and litle wool, much
adoe, and smal help."

Both material and authority for his use of proverbs, and
the other devices he employed for amplification, can be found
earlier in the Adagia, Apophthegmata, and Similia of Erasmus;
but whatever precedents we may find, and whatever may have
been the example of his other contemporaries, without doubt
the main influence upon his style were the precepts and example of his teacher John Rainolds. Rainolds himself was
fond of using proverbs, and he also pointed out in his
Orationes Duodecim that "ea ex historiis, fabulis, carminibus,
autorum dictis, apophthegmatis, similibusque" were pleasing
to learned men and made a gallant show in an oration (p. 432).
In composing his own lectures he practiced what he preached,
and Gosson was his faithful disciple.

iv

What has been said about Gosson's style in the preceding
pages applies only to the first two of his published volumes,

---

17. Elizabethan Proverb Lore (New York, 1926), p. 2.

the Schoole of Abuse and the Ephemerides of Phialo with the
appended Apologie, which were display pieces intended to move
delight and admiration in a general audience. But when three
years later he returned to pamphleteering by publishing Playes
Confuted, the few sparks of moral disapproval which had first
led him to write against the stage had been fanned into flames
of savage indignation as a result of the scurrilous personal
attacks to which he had been subjected. It was not specious
rhetoric but hard logic that he needed to justify his own
position and to destroy the arguments of his adversaries. He
accordingly changed his style completely, and abandoned for-
ever the jingling tintinnabulations of Euphuism.

"Language and Style," said Edmund Bolton, are "the Coat
and Apparel of matter."[18] His sentence epitomizes the Elizabethan attitude toward literary composition; for style at that
time was thought of as external and communal, rather than as
an expression of personality or as individual. It was something to be learned by the study of rules and examples, was
applied from without, not formed from within; so that the
Elizabethan author changed his manner of expression as subject,
audience, or occasion demanded, as easily as a gentleman of
the present changes from tweeds to a dinner jacket.

Gosson explained the change in his own style as follows:

> The righte, for the recovery wherof I framed
> these actions, belongeth not to mee, but unto God,
> whose manner is to beate downe the loftinesse of
> usurpers, not wyth the wisdome of the world or with
> preparation of speare and shield, but with the
> foolishnes of the gospel and the nakednesse of hys
> truth. Therefore, it had bene as daungerous for me,
> in this simple Confutation of our Comedies, to play
> with my penne by seekinge fine pouders for deintie
> noses, as it is for the soldier to dally with his
> weapon when the battle joynes. (*4^V, pp. 160-1)

Depending only upon the "nakednesse of truth"--the compelling
force of logic--he put aside his "fine pouders"--the learned
similes, cumulations of examples, and elaborate sound patterns
of his earlier works--and produced a clear, effective, and
workmanlike prose. He did not write in a manner of absolute
simplicity, such a style would have been almost impossible for

---

18. Hypercritica [c. 1618], printed by J. E. Spingarn,
Critical Essays of the Seventeenth Century (Oxford, 1908), I,
107.

an Elizabethan, but he did abandon the repetitious exuberance
and excessive elaboration of Euphuism.

We have only one example of his pulpit oratory, his sermon
the Trumpet of Warre, published in 1598; from this it is evident that he continued in later life to write a fairly simple
and direct style that was entirely free from the overwrought
ornament of his first two pamphlets. His illustrative examples
were few and were drawn, for the most part, from everyday objects and events or from the Bible. Instead of the references
to Greek and Roman history which he had used in the Schoole of
Abuse and the Ephemerides, to illustrate his arguments he
brought in familiar examples from contemporary events, such as
the price of corn, the late Armada, attempts on the Queen's
life, the "damned crew," etc. He preached from the old pulpit
cross of timber, mounted upon steps of stone, in the churchyard of St. Paul's, where the members of the congregation facing him could look beyond and see the tower of the cathedral
rising two hundred and sixty feet above their heads, and
addressed them with these words:

> When you stand here below upon the ground, and
> looke up to the top of Paules, they that stand upon
> the steeple, appeere small of stature to you, al-
> though they be tall and great, and they that are
> next to you seeme great, by reason of the distance,
> of the one, and the neerenesse of the other: but
> if you stood upon the top of Paules and looked downe,
> they that are above woulde seeme great, and they
> that are beneath woulde seeme little: So is it with
> men in the time of trouble, if their eyes be fastned
> upon the earth, their enemies wil appeare unto them
> to be great and mightie, and God which is so high
> will appeare little. (fol. D5-5ᵛ)

Considering the time, the place, and the circumstances, it was
an effective illustration.

In abandoning the ostentatious symmetry of the Euphuistic
schemes, he was also able to introduce from time to time some
of the periodic rhythm that made the Ciceronian style pleasing
and effective:

> The daies have beene, the question was, What
> shall we bring to the man of God? The daies are now,
> the question is in everie Court of justice, in every
> high court of Parliament, what shall we take from
> the man of God? (fol. F2)

Gosson did not descend to the rude simplicity and dry logic of
the more fanatical Puritans; and he avoided on the one hand the
pedantry of those preachers who esteemed it their "best glorie
to quote an author for every sentence, nay almost every syll-
able," and on the other the strained metaphysical conceits of
the witty preachers who became popular after the turn of the
century. The style of his pulpit oratory was in the best
Anglican tradition, and compares favorably with the work of
Fisher, Jewel, Hooker, and Bancroft.

v

It was not because but in spite of his being a Euphuist
that Gosson's prose still retains some attraction for us today. His nicely balanced and highly patterned sentences quick-
ly become monotonous, and his illustrations, though sometimes
striking and always apt, by their very profusion produce sati-
ety. Even some of the Elizabethans saw the defects of the
style. Sir Philip Sidney, commenting on one of its characteristics, remarked: "For the force of a similitude not being to
prove any thing to a contrary disputer, but onely to explaine
to a willing hearer, when that is done, the rest is a moste
tedious pratling."[19] Euphuism, though it is sometimes amusing,
is too artificial and affected a way of writing to please for
long. It is a blind alley in the history of English prose.

But Gosson, besides being an Oxford student, was also the
son of a Canterbury joiner, and had for three years lived in
London, where he had come in contact with all sorts and conditions of people. So despite the pedantic veneer acquired
during his university days, there continually broke through
into his prose the vigorous and picturesque idioms of the
common people. It is the vivid and forceful colloquialism
of his writing that gives character to his prose and raises
it above the dull and laborious artificiality of the productions of many of his contemporaries.

In the Ephemerides he "useth no going about the bushe,
but treades Dunstable way in all his travell." The players,
he said in the Apologie, "have eaten bulbief, and threatned
highly, too put water in my woortes." Phialo, discouraged by
his misfortunes, sees nothing left but "to sette the hares head
to the goose gyblettes, and al that I have at a mumme chaunce."
In the Schoole of Abuse, Lucinius replying to Augustus "had the
cast to playster uppe his credite" and "flapped him in the

---

19. The Defence of Poesie in Works, ed. A. Feuillerat
(Cambridge, 1922-6), III, 43.

mouth with a smoth lye." Some of his phrases apparently come
from contemporary slang, as when he talks of being "hyssed at
for a blab," or refers to "limme lifters." Note, for example,
the highly idiomatic expression of the following sentence from
the Schoole of Abuse:

> Every Vawter in one blinde Taverne or other, is
> Tenant at will, to which shee tolleth resorte, and
> playes the stale to utter their victualls, and helpe
> them to emptie their mustie caskes. (fol. C2-2ᵛ, p.
> 36)

But the peculiar colloquial character and racy vigor of
Gosson's prose can best be appreciated by means of comparison.
I quote below a passage in the Schoole of Abuse which Gosson
took from Plutarch (Quaestiones Conviviales, VII, viii, 4),
giving first Xylander's Latin version (1572), then Gosson's
own rather free rendering, next Philemon Holland's translation
(1603), and finally Thomas Creech's handling of the same passage in the translation "by several Hands" (1684-94).

> Quod ita scatent scurrilitate et inanitate ver-
> borum, ut ne a puerulis quidem, qui dominis modestis
> calceos portant, spectari ea deceat, quanquam multi
> etiam uxoribus iuxta accumbentibus et impuberibus
> filiis imitationes ostentant rerum et verborum, quae
> magis quamvis ebrietate animos perturbant. (II, 277)

> Plutarch with a caveat keepeth them out, not so
> much as admitting the litle crackhalter that carrieth
> his maisters pantouffles, to set foote within those
> doores: And alledgeth this reason, that those wanton
> spectacles of lyght huswives, drawing gods from the
> heavens, and young men from them selves to shipwracke
> of honestie, will hurte them more, then if at the
> Epicures table, they had nigh burst their guts with
> over feeding. (fol. B4ᵛ, p. 30)

> The other are too ful of ribaudry, of filthy
> and beastly speeches, not wel beseeming the mouthes
> of pages and lackies, that carry their masters
> slippers and pantofles after them, especially, if
> their masters be honest and wise men: and yet many
> there are, who at their feasts, where their wives
> sit by their sides, and where their yoong children
> be present, cause such foolish acts and speeches to
> be represented, as trouble the spirits and disorder

the passions of the minde more, than any drunkennesse
whatsoever. (p. 760)

> And the latter are so full of filthy Discourse
> and lewd actions, that they are not fit to be seen
> by the Foot-boys that wait on civil Masters. Yet the
> Rabble, even with their Wives and young Sons, sit
> quietly to be Spectators of such representations as
> are apt to disturb the Soul more than the greatest
> debauch in Drink. (4th ed., 1704, III, 369)

Grace and polish are not characteristics of Gosson's handling
of Plutarch's words, but force and vigor certainly are. Phrases
like "Crackhalter"--a colloquialism meaning a rogue or a gallows
bird, "shipwracke of honestie," and "burste their guts" give
energy and effectiveness to his expression and contrast favorably with the polite but dull diffuseness of "translator
general" Holland's rendering of the same passage.
    Very few of Gosson's contemporaries had an equal power of
vigorous colloquial expression. Lyly certainly did not have
it, Lodge lacked it entirely, Pettie and Greene rarely achieved
it. Nashe, the Elizabethan master of invective in prose, some
of the Marprelate satirists, and Thomas Deloney were among the
very few who equalled or surpassed him. The bold imagery and
vivid phrasing of colloquial speech was one of the most vital
sources of Elizabethan literary expression; Gosson made an
important contribution when, by his example, he helped to
acclimatize this speech on the printed page.

CHAPTER VI

LEARNING AND SOURCES

i

Some years ago Mr. Parker Woodward observed that the works
signed with the name of Stephen Gosson were written by "an
exceptionally learned man,"[1] and from this he drew what was to
him the inevitable conclusion, that they came from the pen of
Francis Bacon. Despite the absurdity of Mr. Woodward's argument, a part, though only a small part, of his initial assumption is correct. Gosson, for his time, was a learned man. He
had a sounder firsthand knowledge of certain of the classics
than did the general run of university graduates who were his
contemporaries; he was better acquainted with the ancients than
were Greene, Lodge, Nashe, or even Lyly. On the other hand,
he cannot be called exceptionally learned. He had nothing
approaching the breadth of knowledge of a literary amateur
like Sidney, the thorough linguistic training of a teacher
like Ascham, or the breadth of erudition of scholars like Henry
Savile and William Camden. His learning was somewhat above the
average for an Elizabethan, but it was by no means exceptional.
He was able to read at least three languages: English,
Latin, and Greek. He had been taught Latin even before he
entered grammar school, and at Oxford he had been required to
perform all his academic exercises in that language. Like most
other university students of his time, he could probably read
Latin almost as easily as he could read English. The literary
and historical references in his own compositions are drawn almost without exception from works originally written in Latin
or available in Latin translations. He also had at least some
acquaintance with Greek, for that language was part of the
curriculum of the King's School at Canterbury, and he later
studied under John Rainolds, who was the Greek Reader of Corpus.
He once quoted a sentence in Greek from Maximus Tyrius, and he
occasionally used a Greek word; but he apparently seldom did
more than refer to a particular passage in a Greek text, and
preferred to read his Greek authors in Latin translations.[2] He

---

1. Tudor Problems (1912), p. 75.
2. Proof of this is found in an anecdote in the Schoole
of Abuse (fol. A4ᵛ, p. 22): "Anacharsis beeing demaunded of a

quotes Plutarch, for example, in Latin (Schoole of Abuse, fol.
E8, pp. 56-7).

There is no evidence that he could read any of the vulgar
tongues except his own. He once used a French phrase--"a becke
is as good as a Dieu garde"--but that was in a proverb and is
no proof that he knew the language. It is fairly certain that,
in his pamphleteering days at least, he did not know Italian.
In the Apologie he remarked that, though Aristonicus the musici-
an had been honored by Alexander the Great, "this was not done
for sounding Les guanto spagniola, or inventing sweete measures
or coyning newe daunces" (fol. L6^v, p. 69). Obviously he intended "les guanto spagniola" to mean "Spanish song"or"Spanish
songs;" but to be properly written in Italian, his phrase should
have been "il canto spagnuolo" or "i canti spagnuoli." He
placed the plural form of the French definite article before
the singular form of an Italian noun meaning glove (not song);
and after this noun, which is masculine, he placed an adjective
with a feminine ending that is spelled in a manner not to be
found in any language. Gosson wrote a remarkably legible hand,
and the Apologie was very carefully printed; so we can hardly
blame the printer for the errors. These mistakes make it
fairly evident that in 1579 he knew nothing whatever of Italian,
or of French either. He may have picked up a smattering of
these languages later on his journey to Rome, though he could
have made himself understood on the Continent with Latin alone.
There is nothing in his works to show that he had any acquaintance with French or Italian literature.

What is particularly strange is that in gathering material
for his own compositions he apparently never drew upon a single
work written in English.[3] Both Northbrooke and Mundy had written at length against the stage; yet Gosson never once took a

---

Greeke, whether they had not instrumentes of Musicke, or Schooles
of Poetrie in Scythia, answered, yes, and that without vice."
The anecdote comes from the seventh of Maximus Tyrius's Sermones, the Latin translation of which in Stephanus's edition
(Paris, 1557, p. 59) reads: "Interrogatus Anacharsis ab homine
Graeco, num Scythae tibiarum usu haberent, respondit, Ac ne
vitium quidem." Evidently Gosson took "vitium," the geni-
tive plural of "vitis," the word for grape vine, for the accu-
sative singular of "vitium", the word for vice. The confusion
could not have occurred if he had been reading the Greek text,
which has (p. 44) the unmistakable form "ampeloi".

3. Lodge's charge, if it is true, that in Catilins Conspiracies he plagiarized a speech from a play by Thomas Wilson,
indicates an exception to his usual practice. In the Schoole

sentence, an argument, or an illustration from their works.
Other attackers of the stage borrowed freely from one another,
and later writers took considerable material from Gosson; but
he himself mentioned no English author by name except Lodge,
and no influence whatever of any English work can be found in
his writings.

His reading seems to have been confined almost entirely to
Latin, and even among works in that language he seems to have
paid little attention to books by his contemporaries. He had
some acquaintance with the writings of four men who had lived
earlier in the sixteenth century; but they were commentators
on still earlier works. In Playes Confuted he took some materi[a]
from the notes in J. L. Vives's edition (1522) of St. Augustine
De Civitate Dei, and in the same work he also referred to Fox
Morcillo's Compendium Ethices Philosophiae (1554), which is
largely a commentary on Aristotle's Ethics. In the Ephemerides
he may have taken two or three paragraphs from Joachim Cureus's
Libellus Physicus (1567). In the Trumpet of Warre he used a
few arguments from the comments in Cajetan's edition (1507) of
St. Thomas Aquinas's Summa Theologiae. But in proportion to
his borrowings from other sources, he took relatively little
from these books. The works he referred to most frequently,
and from which he drew the greater part of the material for his
own compositions, were those of the ancient philosophers and
historians.

He was not averse to parading his learning, and a person
unacquainted with Elizabethan customs in making references might
assume at first sight that he had a very considerable knowledge
of the classics. In the Schoole of Abuse he mentioned forty-
five authors by name; he referred to twenty-eight of these as
if he were acquainted with their writings, and either quoted

---

of Abuse (fol. C8ᵛ, p. 42) he mentioned Marcus Aurelius's
"Epist. 12. ad Lambertum," a reference to one of the epistles
in Antonio de Guevara's Relox de Principes. There is no evidence that he took any other material from Guevara, so this
single mention may have been drawn from some secondary source;
but if it was made at first hand, the form of the reference
would indicate that Gosson had been reading the work in a Latin
translation, and not in the original Spanish or in the English
versions made by Berners and North. It may be that he even
preferred to read works in the European vernaculars in Latin
rather than in English translations. He occasionally mentioned
the title of an English work--a few plays, the Palace of
Pleasure, etc.--but he drew no material for his pamphlets
from them.

or made direct reference to the works of twenty-three. But more
of this was show than substance; his information about the works
of more than half the authors he mentioned was all at second
hand. But in doing this he was only following the usual custom
of his contemporaries.

I have identified the immediate source of almost every one
of Gosson's literary references. From this investigation it
appears that he was acquainted at first hand with the following
works (the order in which they are listed indicates their relative importance as his sources): Plutarch's Moralia; Xiphilinus's
epitome of Dio Cassius's Roman History; Maximus Tyrius's Ser-
mones; Cicero's Tusculan Disputations, Pro Sexto Roscio Amerino,
Pro Caelio, Ad Familiares, and De Officiis; Lactantius's Divine
Institutes; the Bible, especially the New Testament; Seneca's
Moral Essays and Epistles; St. Augustine's De Civitate Dei with
Vives's commentary; Sallust's Conspiracy of Catiline and
Jugurtha; Tertullian's De Spectaculis and De Corona Militis;
Ovid's Metamorphoses and Ars Amatoria; Aristotle's Nichomachean
Ethics and probably also the Politics; Virgil's Aeneid and
Eclogues; St. Thomas Aquinas's Summa, edited by Cajetan
(Tommaso de Vio); St. Cyprian's Letters; Fox Morcillo's Com-
pendium Ethices Philosophiae; and Xenophon's Cyropaedia and
possibly also his Symposium. In addition he had probably read
Horace's Epistles, Peter Martyr's Commentary on Judges, Calvin's
Commentary on the Psalms, Cureus's Libellus Physicus, and
possibly parts of the works of Plautus, Terence, Martial, Lucan,
Florus, and Persius. Though this list does not indicate an
exceptionally wide range of reading, it is nevertheless a very
respectable one for an Elizabethan.

He apparently read Augustine, Tertullian, and Cyprian for
the specific purpose of composing Playes Confuted. Most of the
other authors he had read in school or at the University; he
seems to have been largely guided by his teachers in his choice
of books. One exception to this is Cajetan's edition of Thomas
Aquinas's Summa, which he used in the Trumpet of Warre, and
which was a work that both Rainolds and Hooker regarded with
disapproval. It may appear strange that an orthodox Anglican
clergyman advocating war against Spain and opposition to the
Roman Catholic Church should have drawn his arguments from a
treatise by a Catholic theologian and from the commentary of a
Spanish cardinal; but English Protestants frequently pillaged
Catholic works of material which they converted to their own
purposes. Gosson may have used St. Thomas and Cajetan in order
to confute the Catholics and the Spaniards out of their own
mouths.

In addition to the books that he studied, the academic
lectures that he listened to are equally important in the con-

sideration of Gosson's sources. Unfortunately, it is not possible to determine the influence upon him of what he heard with as much precision as the influence of what he read. The only lectures of his teachers that survive are those by Rainolds, and we have only fifteen of those, only eleven of which have been printed.[4] But even these few are enough to show that Gosson listened to them attentively and made their contents his own. University students were required to take careful notes at lectures they attended, and had to pay a fine if they did not do so. Evidently when Gosson came to London, he carried with him a large commonplace book filled with jottings taken down while he listened to Rainolds. In Chapter I of this study I showed that many of the general ideas in Gosson's writings came from Rainolds's lectures. In addition, merely from the eleven lectures by Rainolds that have been printed, it is possible to find more than thirty passages which parallel, sometimes even in details of phrasing, specific statements in Gosson's works.[5] It is clear that the most significant formative influence on his intellectual development was his training at Corpus.

The relative importance of the works listed as sources for Gosson's writings can be shown by an analysis of the Schoole of Abuse, almost every paragraph of which is dependent in some way upon a specific literary original. In it he was indebted to Plutarch in fifty-four passages, to Dio Cassius in twenty,

---

4. Two of Rainolds's lectures, Orationes Duae, were published in 1587; nine more were printed in the collection entitled Orationes Duodecim (1614). Four others, still unpublished, are extant in manuscript in Queen's College, Oxford.

5. In the references that follow the title, signature of the first edition, page number in Arber or Hazlitt's reprints of Gosson's writings, and a guide word are given first, then a page reference to the 1619 edition of Rainolds's Orationes Duodecim. Schoole of Abuse *7 (18) Theodorus, 10; A2 (20) poets, 202 and 308; A2 (20) Syrens, 43; A2^V (20) Plato, 88; A3^V (21) Hercules, 330 and 427; A6^V (24) Nile, 285; A8^V (26) Chiron, 289; B-B2 (27) musick, 338 and 366; D5^V (46) Adders, 464; D8^V (49) Souldiers, 447ff; E (50) Capua, 450; E2 (51) common wealth, 413; E4 (53) Pythagoras, 403; F2^V (59) Cephalus, 219. Ephemerides A5 Barrel, 467; B^V Socrates, 466; B3 Amaltheaes, 219; D2 Phoenix, 213; E8 Proteus, 131; E8 Alcibiades 386; G5 Chameleon, 198 and 386; K3^V Phaeton, 323. Apologie L2^V (65) Kings evil, 201; L5 (68) lasciva est, 158; L5^V (68) Antaeas, 264; L7 (70) Hic labor, 374; L7 (70) Plutarch, 338; M3 (74) Patroclus, 334. Playes Confuted C6^V (181) Schoolemaister, 154; D3 (186) Socrates, 63; E7^V (199) Cato, 318.

and to Maximus Tyrius in thirteen. A few of the illustrations
and many of the important ideas can be traced back to Rainolds's
lectures. These four account for about four-fifths of the
derivative material in the essay. The remaining one-fifth,
being something over twenty references and illustrative examples
in all, comes from Cicero's Tusculan Disputations, Ovid's Ars
Amatoria and Metamorphoses, Sallust's Jugurtha and Conspiracy
of Catiline (Gosson had earlier written a play entitled Catilins
Conspiracies), and a small part that cannot be assigned to any
specific source. It would be foolish to assume, without additional evidence, that commonplaces like references to Plato's
expulsion of the poets or to Homer's moly were taken directly
from the Republic or the Odyssey.

Gosson was most indebted to the collection of eighty essays
by Plutarch that have been given the collective title of Moralia.
This is no more than we should expect, for next to Cicero there
is no other ancient author who exerted a greater influence on
sixteenth-century thought and expression. His works are a
storehouse of pithy sayings, witty anecdotes, and apt comparisons,
and there is a hardly a subject of discussion for which he does
not offer some pertinent illustration or some illuminating
comment. Take away the quotations, anecdotes, and other material
Gosson derived directly from Plutarch, and you take away more
than a third of the bulk and some of the best of the content of
his writings.

Gosson must have read and reread the Moralia, for he borrowed copiously from about thirty of the eighty essays and took
occasional passages from some of the others. The De Musica
provided him with all of the material for his attack on music
in the Schoole of Abuse, and the Quaestiones Conviviales much
of his argument against stage plays in the same work. His
treatise on how to rebuke a friend in the Ephemerides was
based largely on Quomodo Adulator ab Amico Internoscatur, and
many of the details in his portrait of a perfect prince in his
"Canvazado to Courtiers" was taken from De Alexandri Magni
Fortuna aut Virtute. Much of his unnatural-natural history,
which some scholars insist on invariably tracing back to Pliny,
comes from Terrestriane an Aquatilia Animalia Sint Callidiora.
The majority of his witty anecdotes and pithy sayings come
from the Regum et Imperatorum Apophthegmata and the Apophthegmata Laconica.

After Plutarch, Gosson was most indebted, largely for
historical anecdotes, to the Roman History of Dio Cassius.
He did not have access to Dio's text itself, but used the
epitome of books XXXVI-LXXX by John Xiphilinus, which had
been published, with a Latin translation by G. Blanco, in 1551.
Dio was not often read by Englishmen in the sixteenth century;

but Rainolds used him, and it is probably through his offices
that Gosson became acquainted with him.

Rainolds's influence on Gosson's reading is most evident
in connection with Maximus Tyrius, the author who stands third
on the list of those he used most frequently. Maximus was an
obscure Greek Neo-Platonist of the second century A.D. whose
Sermones sive Disputationes XLI were first published, with a
Latin translation, by Stephanus in 1557. Rainolds made new
translations of three of the essays in Latin, which were later
printed at the end of his Orationes Duodecim. With the exception of a single reference in a gloss to Spenser's Shepheardes
Calender, Gosson and Rainolds are the only English authors I
have seen who mention the Sermones in the sixteenth century.

Apparently Gosson read only the first half of Maximus
Tyrius's book; but that half he studied carefully, for he took
numerous illustrations and ideas from disputations IV, VII,
VIII, IX, X, XI, XIII, XV, and XXI. In the Schoole of Abuse
he drew material from Quomodo distinguatur amicus ab adulatore,
Utrum recte Plato de civitate sua expulerit Homerum, Quod bella-
tores civitati utiliores sunt quam agricolae, Sermones optimos
esse qui operibus consonent, and Utrum circulares disciplinae
conferant ad virtutem. In the part of section two of the
Ephemerides that deals with flatterers at court he drew heavily
on Quomodo distinguatur amicus ab adulatore; and in the third
part of the same work, where he discusses the problem of virtue,
he took a good deal from the four essays titled, Qualis fuerit
amatoria ars Socratis.

The other books used by Gosson were for the most part those
he had read at school or college, which shows how profoundly he
was influenced by his education at the King's School and at
Corpus. With the exception of Virgil and Ovid, there are no
poets in the first list given above, and all the prose works
are either moral essays or histories. Rainolds, as has been
mentioned before, was no favorer of the pagan poets, and
instructed his students only in those authors who would be
useful to them in the study of divinity.

The omissions in the list of Gosson's sources are as interesting as the inclusions. There is no Homer. He frequently
referred to passages in the Iliad and Odyssey, but these references all came from Maximus Tyrius or Plutarch. There are no
other Greek poets or dramatists, for though Greek was taught
at the King's School and at Oxford, apparently only the historians and philosophers were read. This explains much about
the general attitude toward the classics in that period. Sir
Philip Sidney was eager to learn Greek, not to read Homer, or
Sophocles, or even Plato, but to be able to read Aristotle's
Ethics and Politics in the original. Plutarch's lives at

first sight appears to be another surprising omission. Gosson
drew heavily upon the Moralia; but he never once took anything
from the Lives, and was apparently unacquainted with the latter
work. It was not until North published his translation in 1579
that the Lives became well known in England, and even then they
were not nearly so popular as the Moralia until after the turn
of the century. Still another interesting omission is the name
of Plato. Gosson on occasion referred to him, quoted him, and
discussed his works; but like many of his contemporaries, his
knowledge of the Greek philosopher was all at second hand.

The most significant omissions, however, are the titles of
the many encyclopedias and compends that were so popular in the
sixteenth century, those "distilled books...flashy things" that
Bacon complained of as such a hindrance to sound knowledge.
Gosson was not content, as were many of his contemporaries, to
hold the eel of science by the tail with index learning. Lodge,
Lyly, Meres, and Nashe rifled works like Erasmus's Similia,
Lycosthenes's Apophthegmata, and Textor's Officina for learned
allusions and quotations; but Gosson made his own collections
of such material by direct reference to the writings of the
ancients themselves—at least, I have not yet come upon convincing evidence that he made use of any commonplace book. This
sets him apart as a person of sounder learning than most of the
pamphleteers of his time.

His range of reading was not especially wide; but that
again was the result of his education, for the Elizabethans
thought that students should not be allowed to "rove in many
awcthors, but fewe should be learned most perfectly."[6] How
perfectly he learned the few authors with whose works he was
acquainted is shown by the way in which he used their writings.
He took minor details from places in which we should least
expect to find them: from Plutarch's De Tuenda Sanitate
Praecepta he learned that "Simonides never repented that he
had held his tongue, but often that he had spoken;" from
Cicero's Tusculan Disputations he got information about the
dogs of Hyrcania; and from Sallust's Catiline he drew material
concerning the schools of gladiators in Capua. His use of
materials in this way shows that he had thoroughly assimilated
the matter of his reading and that he could draw upon it as
he wished from memory.

He read with care, and his citations were usually accurate;
only occasionally did he make a mistake. Reference has been

---

6. Quoted from the statutes for the grammar school at
Sandwich by A. R. M. Stowe, English Grammar Schools in the
Reign of Queen Elizabeth (New York, 1908), p. 116.

made in foot note two to his mistranslation of a single passage
in Maximus Tyrius. In the Apologie, which was hurriedly written
he retold an anecdote about Crassus from Cicero's De Oratore
that was really about Gracchus. In the Schoole of Abuse, probably as the result of a hasty reference to Xiphilinus, he gave
"Prasinus" as the name of an individual when it was really the
title of a group of gladiators.[7] But slight errors of this kind
are rare, and Gosson never made such egregious blunders as Lodge
who could refer glibly to the two poets "Orpheus Muscus, and
Linus," when he should have referred to the three poets Orpheus,
Musaeus, and Linus. Even Sidney, by a quirk of memory, made
the two men Bupalus and Hipponax into a single person, whom he
referred to as Bubonax. The Elizabethans did not often bother
to verify their references; Gosson was more accurate than most.

ii

Apparently Gosson never sat down to write without a collection of books at his elbow. Lodge, in his Reply, taunted him by
saying that without his "volumes of historyes" there would have
been no substance in his pamphlets. "Beleve me yf you had wanted your Mysteries of nature, and your stately storyes, your
booke would have scarce bene fedde wyth matter" (fol. B4). That
his compositions were heavily dependent upon the works of others
was the result of the educational system of his time, of which
he was a typical product. He had been taught in school and in
the University to write Latin orations and essays by translating
paraphrasing, epitomizing, and amplifying the productions of the
ancients, and it was only natural that he should use the same
methods when he came to write in English.

His contemporaries had been instructed in the same ways of
imitation, so that a large part of Elizabethan poetry and prose
consists to a considerable extent of a patchwork of phrases and

---

7. On the authority of Dio Cassius he said (fol. B7[v],
p. 33) that Domitian "loved Prasinus the Cochman so wel, that
for good wil to the master, he bid his horse to supper." He
probably used Dionis Nicaei...Epitome, Joanne Xiphilino authore, et Gulielmo Blanco Albiensi interprete (Paris, 1551),
which gives the anecdote (fol. N4[v]) as follows: "Adeo autem
studebat homini viridi veste induto, cui ex colore eius vestis
Prasinus nomen fuit, ut nostris etiam temporibus locus, ubi
ille currus agitabat, Caianus appelletur. Unum vero ex equis
suis quem Velocissimum nominabat, invitabat ad coenam." The
word "Prasinus" is placed in the margin as a side note to this
passage, which is probably what misled Gosson.

passages culled from earlier writers. Some productions of the
period are not even patchwork, but are nearly straight translation. For example, Lyly's chapter, "Euphues and his Ephoebus,"
in the Anatomy of Wyt is, as R. W. Bond has shown, "a version
of Plutarch's De Educatione Puerorum, part paraphrase, part
translation, abbreviated in places, slightly expanded in others."[8]
Lodge, who accused Gosson of plagiarism, translated more than
half of his Reply to the Schoole of Abuse word for word from the
Praenotamenta, an introductory essay to an edition of Terence,
by the French scholar and printer Badius Ascensius.[9] Needless
to say, neither Lyly nor Lodge made any acknowledgment of his
indebtedness. The idea of literary property was not so fully
developed in the sixteenth century as it is today and a writer
would expect, and would receive, as much praise for a series
of cleverly joined extracts or a fine-sounding paraphrase as
he would for an original composition. Vida could not have
complained that his advice to filch from the ancients was
disregarded. Gosson, however, was more conscientious than many
of his contemporaries, for he never descended to straight
translation and only infrequently indulged in paraphrase. He
frequently went to the ancients for arguments or factual
information, but the form and expression of his work was his
own.

His method of composition seems to have been first to
choose a subject; then to read what Plutarch, or Cicero, or the
other authors with whom he was acquainted had to say about it;
after that to organize his arguments according to the rules for
dispositio, search through his notebooks and the volumes in his
library for additional illustrations and examples; and then to
sit down to write with his books in front of him. Any section
of any one of his pamphlets could be used to illustrate his
method of handling his sources; but as he is chiefly known for
his attack on the stage in the Schoole of Abuse, I shall show
in some detail how the section on players in that work was put
together.

In preparing his attack on the stage Gosson apparently
first read Book VII of Plutarch's Quaestiones Conviviales. The
seventh and eighth questions proposed for debate in that book
were, whether or not flute girls should be admitted as entertainers to a feast, and what sort of music is fittest for a
banquet. In the course of the debate on these questions Old
Comedy, New Comedy, and tragedy were discussed. From the

---

8. Lyly, Works, ed. Bond (Oxford, 1902), I, 352.
9. See my article, "The Source of Lodge's Reply to Gosson,"
RES, XV (1939), 364-71.

arguments there brought forward by Plutarch, Gosson built up
the main part of his attack against the Elizabethan theaters.

Gosson preceded his invective against actors with an attack
on musicians. This section of the Schoole of Abuse is made up
entirely of a series of passages taken from Plutarch's De Musica
except for one sentence which is taken from Maximus Tyrius. He
made his transition from the subject of music to the subject of
stage plays by saying:

> For as Poetrie and Piping are Cosen germans: so
> piping, and playing are of great affinity, and all
> three chayned in linkes of abuse.
> Plutarch complaineth, that ignorant men, not
> knowyng the majestie of auncient musick, abuse both
> the eares of the people, and the Arte it selfe: with
> bringing sweete consortes into Theatres, which rather
> effeminate the minde, as pricks unto vice, then pro-
> cure ammendement of manners, as spurres to vertue.
> (fol. B3, pp. 28-9)

The second part of this passage comes from Plutarch's De Musica

> Prisci porro ea ut dignum fuit usi sunt, ut et
> reliquis omnibus institutis. Nostra aetate maiestate
> eius omissa, pro mascula illa et divina confractam et
> garrulam in theatra inducunt musicam. quam Plato III
> De rep. libro vituperata: Lydiam quidem harmoniam
> repudians, ut accommodatam lamentis. (II, 117ᵛ, 23-
> 9)[10]

He then showed (fols. B3-4, pp. 29-30) that Ovid in his Ars
Amatoria (I, 89-100) "planteth his maine battell in publique
assemblies;" that Maximus Tyrius (Sermones, p. 35) held that
"the bringing of instruments to Theaters and plaies, was the
first cup that poisoned the common wealth;" that Romulus "builte
his Theater as a horse faire for hores" (Ovid, Ars Amat., I,
101-34); and that Dio Cassius (LX, 22; LXVIII, 3) rebuked women
for going to theaters. His next three pages (fols. B4-5, pp.
30-1) were taken for the most part from Plutarch's Quaestiones
Conviviales, as can be seen from the following parallels:

---

10. The references here and following are to the volume,
page, and line numbers of Plutarchi Chaeronensis Moralia, Gulielmo Xilandro interprete (Paris, 1572), which contains both the
Greek text and a Latin translation, and was probably the edition
that Gosson used.

The shadowe of a knave hurts
an honest man: the sent of
the stewes a sober matron:
and the shew of Theaters a
simple gaser.

Clitomachus the wrestler geven
altogether to manly exercise,
if hee had hearde any talke of
love, in what company soever he
had bin, would forsake his seat
and bid them adue.

      Lacon when he sawe the
Atheniens studie so muche to
set out Playes, sayde they were
madde.

If men for good exercise, and
women for theyr credite, be
shut from Theaters, whom shall
we suffer to go thither?
Litle children?

Plutarch with a caveat keepeth
them out, not so much as ad-
mitting the litle crackhalter
that carrieth his maisters
pantouffles, to set foote within those doores: And alledgeth
this reason, that those wanton
spectacles of lyght huswives,
drawing gods from the heavens,
and young men from them selves
to shipwracke of honestie,
will hurte them more, then if
at the Epicures table, they had
nigh burst their guts with
over feeding.

Equidem admirationem sui
excitavit Clitomachus
athleta, surgens et dis-
cedens, cum amatorius
sermo inferretur. (II,
275^V, 5-7)

Est vero scitum illud
Laconis, qui, cum
Athenis novi certarent
tragoedi, spectans ap-
paratum choragorum,
studia docentium, et
conatus, dixit: Non
sapere civitatem, quae
tantum in res ludicras
impenderet studium.
(II, 275^V, 18-22)

Sunt ergo, dicebam, mimi,
quorum alii argumenta,
alii ludicra appellantur:
neutrum, ut ego arbitror,
genus convivio conven-
iens...ludicra, quod ita
scatent scurrilitate et
inanitate verborum, ut
ne a puerulis quidem,
qui dominis modestis
calceos portant, spectari
ea deceat, quanquam multi
etiam uxoribus iuxta
accumbentibus et impuber-
ibus filiis imitationes
ostentant rerum et ver-

borum, quae magis
quamvis ebrietate ani-
mos perturbant. (II,
277, 1-10)

For if the body bee over-
charged, it may bee holpe;
but the surfite of the soule
is hardly cured.

Here I doubt not but some
Arch-player or other that
hath read a litle, or
stumbled by chance upon
Plautus comedies, will cast
me a bone or ii. to pick,
saying that whatsoever
these ancient writers have
spoken against plaies is to
bee applied too the abuses
in olde Comedies, where Gods
are broughte in, as Prisoners
too beautie, ravishers of
Virgins, and servantes by
love, too earthly creatures.

De comoediis, vetus ob
inaequabilitatem non
est bibentibus accommo-
data...et levitas con-
viciandi ac acurrilitas
admodum fastidiosa atqu
aperta, et repleta in-
decoris verbis,
lascivisque nominibus.
(II, 276, 35-276^v, 1)

But the Comedies that are
exercised in oure daies are
better sifted. They shewe no
such branne: The first
smelte of Plautus, these
taste of Menander:

Quid dicam de nova
comoedia, quae ita con-
viviis immixta est, ut
facilius ea sine vino:
quam sine Menandro
peragantur? (II, 276^v,
8-10)

the lewdeness of Gods, is
altered and chaunged to the
love of young men; force, to
friendshippe; rapes, to
mariage; wooing allowed by
assurance of wedding; privie
meetinges of bachelours and
maidens on the stage, not as
murderers that devour the
good name ech of other in
their mindes, but as those
that desire to bee made one
in hearte.

Nam neque puerorum amor
in Menandri est comedii
et vitia virginibus ob-
lata, commode in nuptia
vertuntur, meretrices s
introducuntur procaces
et feroces, castigation
bus aut poenitentia
adolescentum amores ear
diffinduntur, si probae
et vicissim amantes:
aut pater alicuius in-
venitur verus, aut temp

amori praescribitur
consuetudinem verecun-
dam humanamque habenti.
(II, 276^v, 19-26)

Nowe are the abuses of the
worlde revealed, every man
in a play may see his owne
faultes, and learne by this
glasse, to amende his
manners.

Haec...ita inter biben-
dum non miror si
iucunditas eorum et
elegantia nonnihil facit
ad effingendum componen-
dumque animos, moresque
ad humanitatem con-
formandos. (II, 276^v,
26-31)

At this point Gosson gave over drawing from Plutarch to
answer (fols. B5^v-6, pp. 31-2) the defense of New Comedy that
had been offered. He referred to Plautus's Curculio and
quoted the first satire of Persius to illustrate the argument;
but replied that "if people will bee instructed, (God be
thanked) wee have Divines enough to discharge that." Then he
quoted Euripides (by way of Plutarch, II, 277^v, 14) on the
foolishness of going to theaters, translated a passage from
Book I of the Quaestiones Conviviales, and continued (fols.
B6^v-7, p. 32) with a long passage from the fifth question of
Book VII as follows:

I cannot thinke that Cittie
to be safe, that strikes downe
her Percollices, rammes up her
gates, and suffereth the enimie
to enter the posterne. Neyther
will I be perswaded, that he
is in any way likely to conquer
affection, which breaketh his
instrumentes, burneth all his
Poets, abandons his haunt,
mufleth his eyes as he passeth
the streate, and resortes too
Theaters too bee assaulted.

Nam neque urbem censen-
dum est capi non posse,
si cum reliquas portas
obicibus, vectibus,
cataractis munitas
habeat, una tamen sit
quae hostes intromittat:
neque invictus a volup-
tate est, quem si non
venus, at musaeum aut
theatrum ceperunt. (II,
271^v, 34-8)

Cookes did never shewe more
crafte in their junckets to
vanquish the taste, nor
Painters in shadowes to
allure the eye, then Poets
in Theaters to wounde the

Nihilo enim minus a via
recta declinavit, ani-
mamque voluptatibus agen-
dum ferendamque prodidit.
Eae vero vehementiora
quam ullus coquus aut

conscience.

There set they abroche straunge consortes of melody, to tickle the eare; costly apparel, to flatter the sight; effeminate gesture, to ravish the sence; and wanton speache, to whet desire too inordinate lust.	unguentarius medicamenta (II, 271ᵛ, 38-272, 2) Magisque varia cantilenarum et rhythmorum ingerentes, his nos capiunt, ac corrumpunt, nostro ipsorum damnatos quodammodo testimonio. (II, 272, 3-5)

There set they abroche
straunge consortes of melody,
to tickle the eare; costly
apparel, to flatter the sight;
effeminate gesture, to ravish
the sence; and wanton speache,
to whet desire too inordinate
lust.

unguentarius medicamenta
(II, 271^V, 38-272, 2)

Magisque varia cantil-
enarum et rhythmorum
ingerentes, his nos cap-
iunt, ac corrumpunt,
nostro ipsorum damnatos
quodammodo testimonio.
(II, 272, 3-5)

Therefore of both barrelles,
I judge Cookes and Painters
the better hearing, for the
one extendeth his arte no
farther then to the tongue,
palate, and nose, the other
to the eye; and both are
ended in outwarde sense,
which is common too us with
bruite beasts. But these by
the privie entries of the
eare, slip downe into the
hart, and with gunshotte of
affection gaule the minde,
where reason and vertue
should rule the roste.

Quare maxime ab huius-
modi cavendum est
voluptatibus. Sunt enim
validissimae; ut quae
non circa gustum, tactum
olfactum, in partem
animi brutam desinant:
sed ipsam intelligendi
ratiocinandique facul-
tatem attingant. (II,
272, 12-16)

The rest of his attack on plays and players (fols B7-C8^V, pp.
32-42) consists of citations of historical examples, largely
drawn from Xiphilinus's epitome of Dio Cassius, and observa-
tions from his own experience, showing the disadvantages which
attended theaters.

It is evident that Gosson handled his sources with a fair
amount of independence. He rearranged the order of topics in
his originals, omitted some arguments, added others, and introduced additional illustrative material from widely different
works. Also, he never followed the exact phrasing of any
author, but always restated what he borrowed in his own words,
giving it increased vividness and force. The merit of his
writings, which for the most part resides in their organization and expression, is his own.

That the details of Gosson's works are so frequently
derived from specific literary originals is in large part the
result of the custom of his times, which demanded that arguments be developed by constant reference to authorities. But

not all of his material comes from literary sources. He had
himself been an actor and playwright, and knew the London
theaters and the plays that were acted in them at first hand.
A great deal of what he has to say, therefore, is the result
of personal observation. His remarks on the productions and
conditions in the London playhouses make his works invaluable
sources of information for historians of the early Elizabethan
drama.

CHAPTER VII

CONTEMPORARY AND LATER INFLUENCE

i

Gosson's active literary career, which is the only part o
his life that remains of interest today, spans a period of not
more than six years of his early manhood. By the time he was
twenty-seven he had written several plays, at least three of
which had been acted on the stage, and he had also published a
few short poems, three pamphlets directed against the newly-
erected theaters, and a work of prose fiction. Few of his con
temporaries succeeded in producing such a quantity or so di-
versified a body of writing while still so young. The number
of items in a man's bibliography is, of course, no measure of
his importance. Gosson, however, did more than produce a
respectable quantity of work; he produced work that is interesting by itself, and that exerted considerable influence on
the thought and writings of his contemporaries. Hitherto his
influence has not been sufficiently recognized.

Gosson's greatest claim to attention depends upon his
connection with the Elizabethan anti-stage controversy. His
own part in that quarrel (represented by the Schoole of Abuse,
the prefatory material to the Ephemerides of Phialo, the
Apologie of the Schoole of Abuse, and Playes Confuted), as wel
as the various replies that his attack immediately called fort
(Straunge newes out of Affrick, Lodge's Reply, the Play of
Playes, the interpolated scenes in the Three Ladies of London,
and Lodge's later remarks in An Alarum against Usurers),[1] have

---

1. A possible further attack is printed by J. O. Halliwell who, in the introduction to his edition of Tarlton's
Jests (1844), quotes a ballad, from a manuscript in the pos-
session of J. P. Collier, entitled "Tarlton's Jigge of a horse
loade of Fooles." The ballad contains what Halliwell remarks
upon as "a curious allusion to Gosson" in the lines (p. xxi):
        This foole he is a Puritane,
            Goose son we call him right,
        A most notorious piebalde foole,
            For sure a hippocrite.

been described in detail in Chapter IV and need only mention here as a reminder of their contemporary importance. The controversies that Gosson's pamphlets stirred up would by themselves demand that literary historians give him their attention.

Of even greater significance, though the results were certainly never part of Gosson's intention, is his influence upon Sir Philip Sidney. Just as Shelley's Defence of Poetry was undertaken in order to refute Peacock's Four Ages of Poetry, so it appears that Sidney composed his Defence of Poesie at least in part as a reply to the Schoole of Abuse. The relationship between the Defence of Poesie and the Schoole of Abuse has been recognized ever since the time of Thomas Zouch, and most scholars since have assumed that Gosson was to a considerable extent responsible for Sidney's undertaking to write his treatise, and that the Schoole of Abuse even determined the course of his arguments. Edward Arber asserted categorically that the Defence was "a carefully prepared answer" to Gosson, and more recently Mona Wilson observed that "several passages in the Defence indicate that the Schoole of Abuse was still fresh in Sidney's mind" when he wrote.[2]

The assertion of Gosson's influence on the Defence, however, has not passed entirely without demur. M. W. Wallace observed that:

> Gosson's name is nowhere mentioned in the Apologie; his book was probably present specifically to Sidney's mind only when he was composing one

---

The lines recall Barnabe Riche's sonnet before the Alarum against Usurers in which he tells Lodge not to fear "Gosse sonne or Ganders hisse." The entire ballad, however, has every appearance of being a Collier forgery—see E. K. Chambers, Elizabethan Stage (Oxford, 1923), II, 342.

2. Zouch, Memoirs of the Life and Writings of Sir Philip Sidney (York, 1808), p. 197; Arber's edition of Sidney's Apologie (1868), p. 7; Wilson, Sir Philip Sidney (1931), p. 156. The same opinion is expressed in introductions to editions of the Defence by A. S. Cook (Boston, 1890), p. xii; E. S. Shuckburgh (Cambridge, 1891), p. xxxiii; and J. C. Collins (Oxford, 1907), p. xxiii. With the exception of Messrs. Addleshaw and Wallace, all of Sidney's recent biographers have also agreed that Gosson's attack provoked the Defence—see the biographies by H. R. Fox Bourne (New York, 1891), p. 205; E. M. Denkinger (1932), p. 159; C. H. Warren (1936), p. 118; and A. H. Bill (New York, 1937), p. 194.

short section of the Apologie--that in which he e-
numerates "the most important imputations laid to
the poor poets." That Gosson was in any sense responsible for Sidney's undertaking to write the
essay there is no reason to believe.

And W. R. Orwen concluded an article on the relations between
Gosson and Sidney with the sentence, "Certainly, Spenser's
hasty assumption that Gosson was 'scorned' by Sidney needs more
substantial proof."[3] But both Mr. Wallace and Mr. Orwen were
led to disagree with the accepted opinion by erroneous evidence.
     Mr. Wallace said that, though the Defence remained in
manuscript until 1595, "it is at least improbable that Gosson
would have dedicated to Sidney the second edition of The School
of Abuse in 1586 [sic] had Sidney's work been generally recognized as a reply to Gosson" (p. 238). Actually the second
edition of the Schoole of Abuse appeared in 1587, after Sidney's
death at Arnheim in October, 1586. Mr. Orwen (p. 575) uses
the same argument, but gives the date correctly. But the second
edition of the Schoole of Abuse can tell us nothing concerning
the later relations of Sidney and Gosson, because Gosson had
nothing to do with issuing it. The second edition was entirely
a publisher's venture, and reprinted the first edition verbatim
with the original dedication unchanged, as was almost always
done in Elizabethan books. The dedication was still addressed
to "Master Philip Sidney," though he had been knighted, and so
had become Sir Philip, in 1583. The epistle at the end was
also still addressed to "Sir Richard Pipe...Lorde Maior of...
London." Sir Richard's term as Lord Mayor expired in October,
1579, and he was never re-elected.
     Mr. Orwen (p. 576) finds evidence of friendly relations
between the two men in the fact that "in 1582 Gosson dedicated
his Playes Confuted in Five Actions to Sidney's new father-in-
law, Francis Walsingham." But in April, 1582, when Playes
Confuted was entered in the Stationers' Register, Sir Francis
Walsingham was not Sidney's "new father-in-law." Negotions for

---

3. Wallace, Life of Sir Philip Sidney (Cambridge, 1915),
p. 238. Orwen, "Spenser and Gosson," MLN, LII (1937), 574-6.
Percy Addleshaw in his biography of Sidney (1909, pp. 359-60),
who admits that the subject confuses him and who is none too
clear in his own statements, appears to doubt whether Gosson
had any effect on Sidney. The only reason he gives is that
"it is hard to realise that the Apologie was specially designed for the refutation of a fool."

Philip's marriage to Walsingham's daughter, Frances, may have been under way then; but they were not public, and the ceremony itself was not performed until September 21, 1583. There is nothing to lead us to believe that Gosson knew of any connection between Sidney and Walsingham in 1582 beyond that of ordinary friendship, and certainly there was no reason for his assuming—or our assuming, for that matter—that Walsingham agreed with Sidney's exalted notions of poetry and the drama (even providing that Gosson knew what those notions were). If we can judge by the literary men to whom we know Walsingham extended patronage, it would appear that he was a favorer of sober historians and theologians, like Hakluyt and Rainolds, rather than of poets and playwrights.

Though the arguments of those who object to the commonly accepted opinion concerning Gosson's influence on Sidney can be disproved, it is still worthwhile to review the positive evidence and decide what conclusions we can legitimately deduce from it. The circumstances, so far as they are known to us, are briefly as follows. On July 22, 1579, the Schoole of Abuse was entered in the Stationers' Register and was published, probably about the same time, with a dedication to "Master Philip Sidney Esquier." In the dedication Gosson said, "I... presente my Schoole, my cunning, and my selfe to your worthy Patronage" (fol. *5^V, p. 17). He said nothing to show that he was personally acquainted with Sidney, he made no mention of former favors received, and he gave no indication that Sidney had in any way authorized the dedication. So far as our information goes, Gosson knew Sidney only by reputation and dedicated his book to him without receiving permission beforehand, which was a perfectly common procedure in the sixteenth century. I have shown earlier, in Chapter II, that the information about Sidney available to Gosson made him a seemingly excellent choice as the patron for a work like the Schoole of Abuse.

About two and a half months later, in a letter to Gabriel Harvey dated from Leicester House, the London residence of Sidney's uncle, the 5 and 16 of October, 1579, Edmund Spenser wrote that "the twoo worthy gentlemen, Master Sidney and Master Dyer...have me, I thanke them, in some use of familiarity." And a few lines farther on he said:

> Newe Bookes I heare of none, but only of one,
> that writing a certaine Booke, called The Schoole of
> Abuse, and dedicating it to Maister Sidney, was for
> hys labor scorned: if at leaste it be in the good-
> nesse of that nature to scorne. Suche follie is it,

not to regarde aforehande the inclination and qualitie
of him, to whome wee dedicate oure Bookes.[4]

Here we have testimony from an associate of Sidney that he
"scorned" the Schoole of Abuse. Sidney's disapproval must be
taken as a fact.
    But only a short time after Spenser's letter was written,
Gosson's second book, the Ephemerides of Phialo, appeared,
again with a dedication to "Master Philipp Sidney Esquier."
Thus, almost at the very time that Spenser was telling Harvey
that Sidney "scorned" Gosson, he had another book in press,
also dedicated to Sidney. In the dedication he referred to the
attacks that had been made upon him as a result of his criticism
of the stage, and said:

> And sith it hath beene my fortune to beare sayle
> in a storme, since my first publishing the Schoole of
> Abuse, and too bee tossed by such as fome without
> reason, and threaten me death without cause, feeling
> not yet my finger ake, I can not but acknowledge my
> safetie, in your Worships patronage, and offer you
> Phialo my chiefest Juel, as a manifest pledge of my
> thankfull heart. (fol. *3-3^V)

This on the surface seems to be a puzzling state of affair
It suggests to Mr. Orwen that Spenser's statement was no more
than a "hasty assumption," and that Gosson actually received
Sidney's patronage (pp. 575-6). But Gosson never said that he
had received any patronage from Sidney. All he said was that
"I can not but acknowledge my safetie, in your Worships patronage." This means, it seems to me: I have been threatened, but
not harmed; I therefore assume that you have exerted your influence on my behalf. If Gosson actually had received some
token of Sidney's approval, he would have made his statement
positive, and not conditional. His dedication in the Ephemerides is as impersonal as that in the Schoole of Abuse. Aside
from the one somewhat ambiguous sentence quoted, he says nothing whatever of Sidney's friendship, favor, or approval.
    Those who are puzzled by the two dedications should re-

---

4. Two Other, very commendable Letters, printed after
Three Proper, and wittie, familiar Letters (1580), fol. G3^V.
The two parts of this volume have separate title pages, but
the signatures run continuously. It was entered on the Stationers' Register June 30, 1580, and is prefaced with an e-
pistle dated June 19, 1580.

member that they were both written within a very short time of
one another. There was only a three-and-a-half months' inter-
val between the entry of the two works on the Stationers'
Register, and the two dedications may have been composed within an even shorter period. We know that when the Schoole of
Abuse was published, the Ephemerides was already in process of
composition (see p. 31). Apparently what happened was as
follows. Gosson chose Sidney as a possible patron and dedicated the Schoole of Abuse to him. Sidney, as we now know,
but as Gosson did not then know, disapproved of the severity
of his attack on poetry, and further disliked the whole method
of the Schoole of Abuse, even the style in which it was written.
There were two courses open to him: he could either rebuke
Gosson privately for his attempt to enlist his support for a
program of which he did not approve or, what was the easier and
at the same time the more gentlemanly thing to do, he could
ignore the whole affair completely. Evidently he chose the
second course, though he did not try to conceal his scorn of
Gosson from his own particular friends. After all, the
dedication had been unsolicited, and he was under no obligation to respond to it if he did not approve of the book.

Also it must be borne in mind that in the late summer and
early autumn of 1579 Sidney was preoccupied with far more important affairs than the conduct of the audiences in the
public theaters. In August Alencon arrived in London, and
Queen Elizabeth showed him exceptional attention. It appeared
certain to almost everyone that she would soon marry him.
Sidney and his friends were bitterly opposed to the match, and
it was apparently at this time that, instigated by Leicester
and others, he composed A Discourse...to the Queenes Majesty
Touching hir Mariage with Monsieur and presented it to Elizabeth. This drew him into the vortex of the political intrigues
of the time. In addition, about the end of August he became
embroiled with the Earl of Oxford over the famous affair at
the tennis court, and it required the intervention of the
Privy Council to prevent a duel between the two. With these
momentous affairs claiming his attention, he could have little
time or inclination to read Gosson's pamphlet and so to find
out specifically what it was about. He may not have examined
it carefully until shortly before Spenser wrote his letter
to Harvey in October, and by that time Gosson's second dedication could have been already in press.

Meanwhile Gosson, uncertain how his first book had been
received, apparently decided to hope for the best, and so
prefaced the Ephemerides with a second dedication to Sidney,
hoping that by doubling his prospective patron's obligation
he would receive a double reward. Spenser's letter reporting

Sidney's sentiments was not made public until the summer of the
following year, and perhaps not until then was Gosson made aware
of his mistake. These deductions provide a perfectly rational
explanation of the two dedications. There is surely no adequate
reason for doubting Spenser's veracity when he reported that
Sidney "scorned" the Schoole of Abuse.

But this leaves still unanswered the second question, concerning the extent to which the Defence of Poesie was a reply
to the Schoole of Abuse. That Sidney nowhere mentioned Gosson
by name in his treatise is no argument against the supposition
that he was the attacker of poetry he had in mind. He found
himself in a difficult position as a result of the dedication.
He did not approve of some of the things Gosson said, yet it
would be beneath his dignity to enter into controversy with
a social inferior, and it would have been a sad breach of
"noblesse and of chevalree"--in which, said Spenser, Sidney was
"president"--for him to attack the man who had asked him for
protection and patronage and had dedicated his book to him as
a token of good will. And yet he owed it to himself to make
his own position clear. Evidently what he decided to do was
to issue no public statement on the subject; but to write an
essay in answer to Gosson's objections in order to make his
own position clear to his personal friends. It is significant
that in beginning the Defence he said he had been "provoked
to say somthing unto you in the defence of that my unelected
vocation" (fol. B^v). The familiar tone of the essay through-
out indicates that it was prepared for his intimates. It
was carefully kept from general circulation and did not appear
in print until 1595, nine years after Sidney's death. It was
also apparently carefully guarded in manuscript, for the
earliest notice we have of its existence dates from 1587, the
year after Sidney's death.[5]

There is abundant evidence in the text of the Defence itself to prove that it was, in part at least, a reply to Gosson.
We know from the Spenser-Harvey correspondence that in the
latter part of 1579 Sidney became interested in the improvement
of English poetry. If he wrote his Defence merely as a result
of these interests, we should expect a formal treatise on the
principles of composition like Gascoigne's Notes of Instruction,
or like the long digression at the end of his own essay in
which he discussed the defects of contemporary poetry and the
methods by which they could be remedied. Or if he was merely

---

5. Academiae Cantabrigiensis Lachrymae, ed. Alexander
Neville (1587), p. 85: "Quid Musis poteras, docuit Defensio
Musae."

impressed with the glorious potentialities of the poetic art
and wished to write something to further it, we should expect
an epideictic composition in its praise, something like
Rainolds's Oratio in Laudem Artis Poeticae. But instead he
said, "I have...just cause to make a pittifull defence of
poore Poetrie" (fol. B^v), and as Professor Myrick has shown,
the artistic form he chose for his defense was the judicial
oration. In other words, he conceived of poetry as brought
to the bar of judgment for certain misdemeanors, and he prepared an elaborate legal brief in refutation of the charges.

It goes without denial, of course, that poetry had been
many times attacked in the sixteenth century before Gosson
published the Schoole of Abuse. Vives, Agrippa, Alley, Ascham,
and Brasbridge are among the many who, in England and on the
Continent, published attacks of one kind or another. That
Sidney was acquainted with works of this kind is shown by
his specific reference to Agrippa (fol. F3). But in none of
these works are all the charges that Sidney answered to be
found. When he took up "the most important imputations laid
to the poore Poets," he summarized the charges under five
headings: (1) poetry is a waste of time; (2) it is the
mother of lies; (3) it is the nurse of abuse, infecting us
with many pestilent desires; (4) it makes us effeminate;
(5) Plato banished poets. In the Schoole of Abuse Gosson
stated that his main objections against poets were those of
Cicero, who "accompted them the fathers of lyes, Pipes of vani-
ties, and Schooles of Abuse" (A3, p. 21). He also said, "I
disprayse his methode in writing, which following the course
of amarous Poets, dwelleth longest in those pointes, that
profite least" (A^v, p. 19). And in another place he said, "No
marveyle though Plato shut them out of his Schoole, and banished
them quite from his common wealth, as effeminate writers, unprofitable members, and utter enimies to vertue" (A3, p. 20).
A comparison of these two lists makes it evident whom Sidney
was answering.

Many passages in the Defence are specific answers to particular arguments in the Schoole of Abuse.[6] To take one example
from among many, Sidney, referring to the attackers of poetry,
says:

---

6. Many of these have been pointed out in the notes to
the editions by Cook and Shuckburgh. Jacob Bronowski, The
Poet's Defence (Cambridge, 1939), pp. 19-56 gives a closely
reasoned analysis of the way Sidney's own theories of poetry
were shaped by his attempts to meet and overcome Gosson's
arguments.

> They alledge herewith, that before Poets began
> to be in price, our Nation had set their hearts de-
> light uppon action, and not imagination, rather doing
> things worthie to be written, then writing things fit
> to be done. (fol. G2ᵛ)

This echoes Gosson's charge that Englishmen had degenerated from
their former greatness as a result of the enervating effects of
poetry and plays. In England "in olde time," Gosson said, we
find:

> The men in valure not yeelding to Scithia, the
> women in courage passing the Amazons. The exercise
> of both was shootyng and darting, running and wrest-
> ling, and trying such maisteries, as eyther consisted
> in swiftnesse of feete, agilitie of body strength of
> armes, or Martiall discipline...But the exercise that
> is nowe among us, is banqueting, playing, pipyng, and
> dauncing, and all suche delightes as may win us to
> pleasure, or rocke us a sleepe. (B8ᵛ, p. 34)

There can be no question that the Defence of Poesie was prepared
as a confutation of the Schoole of Abuse. Gosson was therefore
unintentionally responsible for provoking the most important
critical essay of his century.
        But though Sidney scorned the Schoole of Abuse, he did not
disagree with everything that Gosson had to say. He admitted
the justice of many of his strictures. Comedies, he said,
"naughtie Play-makers and stage-keepers, have justly made
odious" (fol. E4). And in another place he said, "I will not
denie, but that mans wit may make Poesie...infect the fancie
with unwoorthie objects" (fol. G2). Actually, Gosson and
Sidney had fundamentally similar ideas concerning the nature
and function of poetry; but they arrived at almost diametri-
cally opposed conclusions about its place in the state. Because in it good and bad are usually mixed, Gosson would
banish it; because, though it may be abused, it is capable of
doing much good, Sidney would honor it. These two strands of
opinion cross and recross each other, like warp and woof, in
all Elizabethan criticism. There is no better introduction to
both these aspects of sixteenth-century thought about literature than the reading of Gosson side by side with Sidney. Both
epitomize the best that had been thought and said in defense
of their respective positions.

ii

In addition to the replies they provoked, Gosson's writings continued for more than fifty years to influence other opponents of the stage by providing them with arguments and illustrative materials. In 1580, the year after Gosson entered the controversy, Anglo-phile Eutheo (i.e., Anthony Mundy) in his Second and third blast of retrait from plaies and Theaters praised the Schoole of Abuse as "the first blast" against the stage and repeated some of its arguments.[7] Three years later Philip Stubbes drew fully a third of his essay against the theater, printed in his Anatomie of Abuses, word for word from Playes Confuted.[8]

Even in the early seventeenth century Gosson's pamphlets continued to be influential. Henry Crosse, whose Vertues Commonwealth appeared in 1603, devoted about a dozen pages of his book (fols. P2-Q3^v) to an attack on the stage. Crosse was competent enough as a writer not to have to depend on others for the phrasing of his arguments, so there are no verbal echoes of earlier compositions in this part of his work; but he traversed much the same ground that Gosson had covered in

7. Ed. W. C. Hazlitt in The English Drama and Stage (n. p., 1869), p. 99; see also pp. 144, 148. Mundy also took over verbatim several passages of considerable length from Bk. III, chap. vii of a translation by Geoffrey Fenton, A forme of Christian pollicie drawne out of French, which was published in 1574 (the references that follow contain, first, a guide word and page number from Mundy's treatise as reprinted by Hazlitt and, second, a page reference to Fenton): "Sabboth" 128, 145; "first Table" 135, 144; "corrupted with their gestures...dissolute words" 144-5, 144; "principal end...handes" 149, 143; "primitive Church...Cyprian" 150, 144.

8. The following page references are to Hazlitt's reprint of Stubbes and Playes Confuted: "Tertullian...Augustinus" 220, 176; "Scipio" 221, 177; "Valerius maximus" 221, 177-8; "Aristotle" 221, 182; "Venus...Mercurie" 221, 190; "Tragedies ...Commedies" 221-2, 180; "runnyng to...Plaies" 223, cf. Schoole of Abuse C^v. Stubbes drew most of the rest of his material from Northbrooke's Treatise (references are to Collier's edition): "Theopompus...Theodictes" 220, 92; "Pecunias" 220, 85; "Chrisostome" 221, 90; "Lactantius" 221, 92; "Carthage... Laodicea" 221, 90; "Ovid" 221, 93; "Constantius" 221, 97; "Sermons" 222, 93; "light darknesse" 222, 92; "Otia" 222, 60; "Churche...emptie" 223, 94; "learne falshood...deride" 223-4, 94-5; "roagues" 225, 98.

Playes Confuted, used many of the same arguments and illustrations, and may very well have derived some of his material from
him. An even more obvious case of borrowing is found in I. G.'s
A Refutation of the Apology for Actors (1615), a line by line
reply to the treatise that Thomas Heywood had issued three
years previously. I. G. repeats Gosson's criticism of playwrights' tampering with historical truth in arranging their
plots,[9] and devoted the last part of his book (pp. 54-66) to an
orderly discussion of the efficient, material, formal, and
final causes of plays--the topics under which Playes Confuted
was organized. I. G. took over not only Gosson's topics, but
also several details from his arguments.

In 1633 William Prynne issued his Histrio-Mastix, the
Players Scourge, containing more than a thousand closely-print-
ed pages of argument and invective against the plays and
theaters of his time. He opposed the drama on the authority
of, among others, "above 150 foraigne and domestique Protestant
and Popish Authors" who had written since the year 1200, and
as we should expect we find Gosson's Schoole of Abuse and
Playes Confuted frequently cited (see pp. 140-1, 172, 198, 227,
309, 320, 358, 360-3, 436-7, 486, 489, 698, and passim). Like
Gosson, Prynne divided his arguments into "acts," his first
part consisting of eight "acts" and a final "chorus," his second part of five "acts" and a concluding "catastrophe;" he may
very well have got the idea for this method of organization
from Playes Confuted, which was divided into "five Actions."
Prynne also drew many arguments and illustrations from Gosson;
but he was most interested in him because he was "a penitent
reclaimed Play-poet (whose eyes did shed many teares of sorrow,
whose heart sweat many drops of blood, when he remembred Stage-
playes, to which he was once addicted)" (p. 436). At another
place he explained that Gosson was "once a professed Play-poet;
yea a great Patron, and admirer of Playes and Players, as himself confesseth, till God had called him to repentance, and
opened his eyes to see their abominablenesse" (p. 360); and
then he quoted Playes Confuted on the immorality prevalent in
theaters, and remarked in the margin, "Note this: and note it

---

9. P. 42. I. G., whose book is little more than a compilation drawn from earlier treatises, also drew material, frequently verbatim, from Stubbes's Anatomie (pp. 42, 51-2, 55-7,
60, 62, 64), Healey's translation of Vives's edition of St.
Augustine's De Civitate Dei (pp. 19-23, 36, 43); Hoby's translation of Coignet's Politique Discourses (pp. 50-1), North's
translation of Guevara's Diall of Princes (pp. 26, 45-50), and
Polydore Vergil's De Rerum Inventoribus (p. 33).

so as to believe it, because the Author testifieth it from his owne experience" (p. 362). Gosson was without question the star witness in Prynne's case against the stage.

In the encyclopedic work of Prynne we find the last evidence of Gosson's direct influence upon the anti-stage controversy. After the sixteenth century, the Schoole of Abuse was not reprinted until 1810, and Playes Confuted not until 1869. In the seventeenth and eighteenth centuries, therefore, his pamphlets were rare and hard to come by, and so were known to only a few antiquaries. When the attack on the stage was once again renewed by Jeremy Collier with his Short View of the Immorality and Profaneness of the English Stage (1698), nothing of consequence was drawn by the contestants on either side from Gosson or any other Elizabethan, because their works were no longer generally obtainable. George Ridpath, one of Collier's supporters, found references to Gosson in Prynne's Histrio-Mastix, and like Prynne he held him up as an example of a playwright who had realized the error of his ways.[10] But how little authority Gosson's name then carried is shown by the anonymous author of The Stage Acquitted (1699) who replied to Ridpath by remarking:

> This instance of Gosson is not to be depended on, since his Book is not extant, and has nothing but Mr Prynn or R[idpa]th to support its Authority, who pickt up Authors scarce ever heard of before or since. (pp. 139-40)

By the end of the seventeenth century Gosson had so completely dropped out of remembrance that it was even possible to question that he had ever existed.

iii

With the revival of interest in the Elizabethan drama that came about in the eighteenth century, historical studies of the early stage began to appear, and these of necessity gave accounts of the early playwrights and of the attacks that had been made on the theaters. John Strype, in the additions he

---

10. The Stage Condemned (1699), pp. 103, 108. For an account of the controversy stirred up by Collier, see A. Beljame, Le Public et les Hommes de Lettres en Angleterre au Dix-Huitième Siècle (Paris, 1897); J. Ballein, Jeremy Collier's Angriff auf die englische Buhne (Marburg, 1910); and R. Anthony, The Jeremy Collier Stage Controversy (Milwaukee, 1937).

made to Stow's Survey of London (1720; Bk. I, chap. xxix), was
the first eighteenth-century scholar to discuss in any detail
the causes for early opposition to the stage; but he confined
his remarks to the legislative acts of the Common Council of
London. Robert Dodsley, in the preface to his Select Collection
of Old Plays (1744), gave a brief account of the literary aspects of the controversy, and mentioned Gosson's Schoole of
Abuse and Playes Confuted as the two most important treatises
issued by the opposition (I, xxviii). George Chalmers, in his
essay published in the first variorum Shakespeare (1803), "A
Farther Account of the Rise and Progress of the English Stage"
(III, 440-9), discussed the subject in more detail, though it
was not until J. P. Collier devoted the ninth and tenth conversations of his Poetical Decameron (Edinburgh, 1820) to
Elizabethan authors who attacked the stage, that anything
approaching a comprehensive survey of the topic was made available. Collier devoted over twenty pages to Gosson (II, 208-
31). In the present century several specialized studies of
the subject have been published, notably Professor E. N. S.
Thompson's book, The Controversy Between the Puritans and the
Stage (New York, 1903), and now no history of Elizabethan drama,
or even of Elizabethan literature, that pretends to any com-
pleteness can omit an account of the anti-stage controversy
and of the significance of Gosson's contribution to it.

Scholars also soon discovered that Gosson's pamphlets
contained a mine of information concerning the early drama and
the conditions in the first theaters. Richard Farmer found
the Schoole of Abuse useful in his "Essay on the Learning of
Shakespeare" (1767; repr. first variorum Shakespeare, II, 63).
Edmund Malone, in his "Historical Account of the Rise and
Progress of the English Stage" (1790), drew frequently from
both the Schoole of Abuse and Playes Confuted for points of
theatrical history. J. P. Collier also, in his History of
English Dramatic Poetry (1831), took even a greater amount of
material from them. Every historian of the Elizabethan drama
since has found in Gosson's pamphlets valuable source material
for the illumination of his subject--in Sir Edmund Chambers's
Elizabethan Stage (1923), for example, there are twenty-seven
index entries under Gosson's name. Gosson tells us, among
other things, about the salaries of actors, the behavior of
the audiences at performances, the structure of the theaters,
the dramatic construction of early plays, and the sources from
which they were drawn. He mentions by title a considerable
number of plays that are now lost and gives us information
about them. One of these, entitled The Jew, some scholars
think, though it appears to me a very doubtful hypothesis, may
have been the source of Shakespeare's Merchant of Venice. Gos-

son's passing reference in the Schoole of Abuse—"the Jew...
showne at the Bull...representing the greedinesse of worldly
chusers, and bloody mindes of Usurers" (fol. C6^v, p. 40)--
provides us with all the information we have concerning it.

iv

Gosson is usually considered today mainly for his connection with the anti-stage controversy; but that is not the only
thing for which his contemporaries regarded him. It will be
recalled that Lodge predicted that he would be "praised" for
his "stile," and it was as a stylist, as a writer of vigorous,
highly ornamented prose, that the Elizabethans most admired
him. John Lyly, only a few months after the publication of
the Ephemerides, referred with approval in Euphues and His
England to the first book of Gosson's work:

> Hast thou not read since they comming into
> England a pretie discourse of one Phialo, concerning
> the rebuking of a friende? Whose reasons although
> they wer but few, yet were they sufficient, and if
> thou desire more, I coulde rehearse infinite.[11]

Other contemporaries paid Gosson even higher compliments by
borrowing for their own works, without acknowledgment, many of
the most effective passages in the Schoole of Abuse, the
Apologie, and the Ephemerides. Anthony Mundy, in his romance
entitled Zelauto...Given for a freendly entertainment to
Euphues, at his late arivall into England (1580), took over
verbatim in his preface (fol. *3^v) a passage of comparisons
from the Schoole of Abuse (fol. C4^v, p. 38). Brian Melbancke
was evidently a great admirer of the Ephemerides and Apologie
as well as of the Schoole of Abuse, for he borrowed profusely
from them in over thirty passages of his work of prose fiction
entitled Philotimus, the Warre betwixt Nature and Fortune
(1583).[12] The name of his hero, Philotimus, is obviously taken

---

11. Works, ed. R. W. Bond (Oxford, 1902), II, 99. It
would seem that Lyly was a trifle put out with Gosson's compe-
ting with him in his own field, and though he had to admit the
merit of the Ephemerides, nevertheless could not forbear from
boasting that he could do better.

12. R. B. McKerrow, Works of Nashe (1910), IV, 481, was
the first one to remark that "Melbancke was evidently familiar
with Gosson's work." He pointed out that Melbancke, p. 14,
took over the anecdote concerning "Tyresias" from the Ephemeri-

from Philotimo, Phialo's friend in the Ephemerides.

Melbancke's romance furnishes an interesting example of
the devious channels through which the tide of Euphuistic influence flowed. His book, which though published in 1583 was
according to his own account composed at least a year and a
half before that date, contains many pages of typically
Euphuistic prose. Yet Melbancke was a Cambridge graduate, and
so probably had no opportunity to listen to Rainolds's lectures;
and though he was a notable plagiarist, I have not noticed that
he borrowed anything from Euphues or Euphues and His England.
Evidently he learned his Euphuism from Gosson, and not from
Lyly.

Later Thomas Nashe, in his Anatomy of Absurdity (1589),
also borrowed from the Ephemerides.[13] But the best indication
of the esteem Gosson's contemporaries held him in as a stylist
is the inclusion of several quotations from his works in a
volume entitled Politeuphuia, Wits Commonwealth (1597). Nicholas Ling, the publisher, described this book in his dedication
as "a methodicall collection of the most choice and select
admonitions and sentences" from the best ancient and modern
authors. Passages from Gosson's works are given an equal place
beside passages from Sir Philip Sidney and John Lyly.[14]

---

des, fol. B8. H. E. Rollins, "Notes on Brian Melbancke's
Philotimus," SP, extra series I (1929), 48, showed that Melbancke, p. 36, borrowed the anecdote of the bath keeper's ass
from Gosson's Apologie, fol. M[v]. More recently D. C. Allen,
"Melbancke and Gosson," MLN, LIV (1939), 111-14, noted sixteen
additional parallels. But the investigations of these scholars have not exhausted the catalogue of Melbancke's indebtedness to Gosson. The following list indicates still another
sixteen parallels, and more might possibly be found: "Aristotle" Melbancke p. 26, Eph. fol. A8; "Caligula" 36, Eph. F;
"Calidon" 36, Eph. F4; "Heraclitius" 38, Eph. A3[v]; "clarke...
Amaltheas" 38, Eph. B3; "Juno" 46, Eph. *7[v]; "Dieugarde" 46,
Eph. C5; "nourishmente...lookes" 49, Eph. G5; "Carthaginians"
77-8, Schoole D7; "waterman" 114, Eph. K6; "Germany" 136, Eph.
H6[v]; "Beares" 146, Eph. *7; "Clearchus...Domitianus" 170, Eph.
D4; "bulbeefe...kine" 171, Apol. L[v]; "pad" 172, Eph. A3. Mel-
bancke's "Well in Illirica," "river in Pontus," and "River
Lycus" (pp. 147-8) are from Fortescue's Foreste (1571, fol.
90-90[v]). There are numerous additional borrowings from many
other works.

    13. See McKerrow's notes, Works of Nashe, IV, 481-2.
    14. Gosson's name is never mentioned, but the passages
are easily recognized by anyone well acquainted with his writ-

In all likelihood other writers also drew upon Gosson's
works for both phrases and ideas. Though I have not investi-
gated the matter, it seems impossible that Greene, for example,
should have left so promising a source unplagiarized.[15] If we
leaf through sixteenth-century editions of Gosson's works, we
notice that the Elizabethan readers have underscored many
passages and written notes in the margin. Almost invariably
their markings call attention to sententiae, striking comparisons, or passages of elaborately schematic prose;[16] it is clear
that these readers admired his style. From this and what has
been said on the preceding pages, it is evident that Gosson
was recognized in his own time as something more than a controversialist, that he exerted a significant influence on both
the prose style and the content of contemporary works of
fiction.

v

When we survey Gosson's career, we find that his progress
was slow but steady, bringing him ever greater material prosperity and social distinction. Beginning as the son of a
humble Canterbury joiner, he rose to be the rector of the
richest and one of the most important London churches. Though
high positions in the Church have always been open to men of
ability, regardless of their social origin, his advancement is
nevertheless an index to the period of social upheaval and
economic expansion that began under the Tudors, when the new
middle class came into being and grew rapidly in wealth and
influence.

---

ings. The numbers that follow refer to the folios of the second, 1598, edition of Politeuphuia: "Myll" 166, Eph. B2^V-3;
"Swallowe...silver" 166^V, Schoole A5; "surfit" 167, Schoole
B4^V; "heaven" 167, Schoole C4^V; "mighty" 167^V, Schoole E2;
"cloude" 167^V, Schoole E4^V; "marks" 167^V, Schoole F2; "Cephalus" 167^V, Schoole F2^V; "words...deeds" 180^V, Schoole D3;
"Faire faces" 242, Eph. G7^V.

15. I have noticed a possible parallel here and there--
cf Carde of Fancie (Everyman ed.), p. 237; Schoole of Abuse,
fol. *3, p. 16.

16. The Princeton University Library copy of the Ephemerides (1579) is especially interesting in this respect. It
was once the property of Sir Robert Gordon of Gordonstoun
(1580-1656), who wrote his name on the title page. For a description of the notations in this copy, see my account in
the Princeton Library Chronicle (1942).

Gosson hardly deserves a place in the first, or even in
the second rank of writers of his time; but he had talent, a
ready wit, a good education, and he used them intelligently.
He was the most influential of the early opponents of the
stage, he made some contribution to the still undeveloped art
of prose fiction, and he played an important part in introducing and popularizing the new prose style called Euphuism.
His most significant artistic accomplishment, however, was his
vigorous colloquial prose. No account, certainly of Elizabethan
criticism, even of Elizabethan literature in general, would be
complete without some consideration of his writings.

But it is because of what he represents, rather than because of what he actually accomplished, that he has an importance greater than that of some of his more original and
more talented contemporaries. He epitomizes, in both his life
and his writings, the ideals of the new Elizabethan middle
class, and he thus stands as the spokesman for an important
group whose members were for the most part inarticulate. He
was a sturdy conservative; "I be of Plutarches opinion," he
said, that "the oldest fashion is ever best." He was an en-
thusiastic nationalist and patriot; he admired "the olde
discipline of Englande," and was solicitous for its present
strength and welfare. He had a firm respect for properly
constituted authority and approved the Tudor absolutism; but
he insisted that the function of government was to serve the
people. He abhorred extravagance and idleness, and considered
thrift and industry as primary virtues; one of his main charges
against the theaters was that to attend them was a waste of
time and money. His criterion of values, both for art and for
life, was largely based on considerations of utility; he
attacked poets because they were "uselesse" members of a
commonwealth, and he wanted to banish plays because they did
not provide "profitable recreation." Finally, he was sincerely
religious and was a staunch upholder of social morality; he
inveighed against certain activities because he considered
them "utter enemies to vertue." These are typically bourgeois
ideals that were receiving renewed emphasis in the sixteenth
century.[17]

Gosson represents, then, not the England of the Earls of
Oxford and Essex, of exquisite gentlemen and daring soldiers;
but the England of the steady, sober, God-fearing merchants
and artisans, the men who were slowly bringing about a new
order. Gosson wrote on the same subjects as the courtly

---

17.   See L. B. Wright's Middle-Class Culture in Elizabethan
England (Chapel Hill, 1935).

writers, but he gave expression to the middle-class point of
view. If his remarks on poetry and the drama are compared to
the theories of Sidney, if his discussion of neo-Platonic
notions of love is put beside the treatments of the same subject in the sonnet sequences and court masks, and if his
portrait of the ideal courtier is examined in connection with
Spenser's presentation of his ideal in Sir Calidore, a complete
rather than partial picture of Elizabethan thought and opinion
will result. Only with a knowledge of both points of view is
an adequate understanding of the Elizabethans possible.

APPENDIX A

BIOGRAPHICAL DOCUMENTS

I. Letters

(i) To the Archdeacon of St. Albans, November 18, 1590.
See above, Chapter III, pp. 45-6.

(ii) To Edward Alleyn, September 29, 1616. Dulwich
College MS., III, 92 (autograph). Printed by William Young,
The History of Dulwich College (1889), I, 31. The name that
Young prints as "Raphe Snider" I read as "Raphe Pinder."

(iii) To Edward Alleyn, October 2, 1616. Dulwich College
MS., III, 94 (autograph). Printed by J. P. Collier, Memoirs
of Edward Alleyn (1841), pp. 133-4.

(iv) To Edward Alleyn, August 7, 1617. Dulwich College
MS., III, 103 (in the hand of Raphe Pinder):
            To the worshipfull Edward Allin Esquire.
After our very harty commendations. wee the parson and parishioners of the parish of St Buttolph without Bishopsgate London.
whose names are heerunder written. doe heerby certefye you. that
as formerly wee are obliged unto you for your Benevolence Al-
readye extended to some of our poore parishioners. so now (by
your further Bountye Imbouldened) accordinge to your prescriptio
wee (with due Consideration) have made choyce of three children
in our sayd parish whom (for gods cause) wee doe Intreat you
to accept of. into your Schoole. ther to manifest your works
of mercy upon them. to the glory of god. your owne credit. and
ther comfort. The first of them is one Richard Merrydall about
10 years ould. the which childe is both fatherlesse and mother-
lesse. the Second is Simon Waddup about 8 years of age. whose
father is both very lame and past his labour. the third is one
Thomas Shippey the sonne of a woefull and a distressed widdow
and some 8 years oulde: of the which children may it please you
to make acceptance. we shall. (and they much more) bee Ever
bounde to prayse god. for his goodness toward them. extended
by you. of whom in most Intyre love. wee take our leave. this
7th of August Anno. 1617. Restinge.
                    Your worships very loveinge ffreinds

[Signed]   Steph Gosson Rect
                            Raphe Pinder Depeutt
                            Thomas Dunnyng
                            Wm Whittwell   ) Churchwardens
                            Dominick Comely)

(v) To Edward Alleyn, September 1, 1617. Dulwich College
MS., III, 106 (in the hand of Raphe Pinder). Printed by Young,
op. cit., I, 36; Collier, op. cit., p. 135.

(vi) To Edward Alleyn, March 17, 1621/2. Dulwich College
MS., III, 126 (in the hand of an amanuensis):
To the worshipfull mr Edward Allin Esquire from the parishioners of the parish of St Butolph without Bishopsgate London this
17th day of March 1621 Sir According to your direction in
those Articles which your worshipp sent and directed unto us
lately wee have Ellected 4 poore children viz:
1 Randall the sonn of John Sparrow Sexton of this parish having
vi small children
2 John the sonn of Nicholas Sparkes A widower A very mizerable
poore man having 4 small children and no Nurse but himselfe to
suker them
3 Thomas the sonn of Henery Heyes A very poore man, having vi
small children
4 Robert the sonn of Thomas Brounrigg A very poore man having
4 or 5 small children
Divers other made great sute to be prefered to your charetie but
by Lott those wear dissmised and theis presented Acording to
your own Custom thus Desyring the Lord to Add blessings uppon
yow for theis works of mercy wee take our leave the day and
yeare abovsaid
            [Signed]   Steph Gosson Rector
                                 Raphe Pinder
Bartholomew Foster   Thomas Dunnyng
Samuell Fford   Wm Whittwell
Richard Cowlay   John Day   ) churchwardens
the marke of M mr Hoby   Robart Osborn)
                                 John Pywell

II. Will of Stephen Gosson

In the name of God Amen the ffather the sonne and the holye
Ghoste three glorious persons in the blessed trinitye and one
eternall god in substance, to whome be ascribed all honour and
Glorye for ever Amen I Stephen Gosson Rector of the parrish
Church of St Buttolphe without Bishops gate London beinge in
perfecte health of bodye, and sound sences and perfecte memorye,

this fyve and twentieth daye of November Anno domini 1622 and
in the twentieth yeare of the Raigne of our Soveraigne Lord
King James of England &c. do make this my last will and testament (revokeing all other wills and testaments by me formerlye
made) in manner and forme followeing Imprimis I render up my
soule when yt departeth out of my bodye and I bequeath yt into
the hands of my Lord and Saviour Jesus Christ who redeemed me
and all the sonnes and daughters of Adam with the inestimable
price of his most holye bloud shedd for me and for all man
kind uppon the Crosse, trustinge to receive remission of all
my sinnes by his death and passion and by his meritts not by my
owne, Alsoe I bequeath my bodye dust and ashes to be buryed in
the Channcell of the said parrish church of St Buttolphe a
foresaid, there to be layd nere my well beloved wiffe Elizabeth Gosson, and Elizabeth my daughter, and to be kept there
in the storehouse of the faithfull untill the generall res-
urrection, And as touchinge that porcion of worldlye substance
where with god hath blessed me I dispose of that in this manner,
ffirst I doe give to my welbeloved sister Dorothye Mansworth
(the wiffe of William Mansworth) of newe Castle ffiftye pounds
lawfull money of England, Item I doe give and bequeath unto my
welbeloved neece Dorothye Mansworth ffiftye pounds lawfull
money of England, Item I doe give to the poore of the parrish
of Stanbridge in the Countye of Hartford nere St Albans where
I was first beneficed fortye shillinges of lawfull money of
England, And to the poore of the parrish of greate Wiggborrowe
in the County of Essex ffortye shillinges of like money, Item
I doe give unto the poore of the parrish of St Buttolphe without Bishops gate where I was laste beneficed fyve poundes of
lawfull money of England, the same fyve poundes to be distributed in this manner followeinge That ys to saye unto two
hundred poore Parishioners sixe pence a peece, And to be
delivered unto them by the handes of my brother William Gosson.
Item I doe give and bequeath to the poore of the parrish of
Stebamheath [i.e., Stepney] where I was a lecturer before I
was beneficed twentye shillinges, and to the poore of the
parrish of St Martyn Ludgate hill London, where I was also a
lecturer before I was beneficed the like somme of twentye
shillinges, Item I doe give and bequeath to my maid servannt
Marye Judkin three poundes of lawfull money of England over
and above her wages Item I do give to Mr Dunvell my Curate
ffiftye shillinges Currante money of England. Item I doe give
to Paule Bassano tenn shillinges to buye him a paire of gloves
Item I doe give to my Cozen Margaret Oxenbridge ffiftye
shillinges Item I doe give to my Clarke Richard Wylye Twentye
shillinges to my Sexton Sparrowe Tenn Shillinges. The rest
and residue of all and singuler my goodes Cattelles Chattelles

[sic] plate household stuffe whatsoever I doe give and bequeath unto my Loveinge Brother William Gosson, And I doe nominate make constitute and appoynte the said William Gosson my brother the full and sole Executor of this my last will and testament And I doe make Anthonye Jeffes my overseer and I doe give to the same Anthony tenn shillinges In wittnes whereof I the said Stephen Gosson have hereunto sett my hand and seale By me Stephen Gosson Sealed Subscribed pronounced and delivered by the said Stephen Gosson for his last will and testament the fyve and twentieth daye of November 1622 in the presence of vs. Ro. Dumvile and Richard Rochdale scrivener.
Proved at London, February 16, 1623[/4], by William Gosson, brother of the deceased and executor. (145 Bellamy, Consistory Court, London).

III. Records Concerning William Gosson

Note. There were several William Gossons living in the late sixteenth and early seventeenth century. The following extracts are taken only from those documents that can be proved to refer to Stephen's brother.

(i) Christenings: March 28, 1558. Will'm, son of Cornelius Gosson (Register of St. George's, Canterbury, ed. Cowper).

(ii) November 23, 1599. Grant to William Gosson, the Queen's drum player, in place of Thos. King, lately deceased, of the fee of 12d a day and £16 2s 6d for his livery (State Papers Dom., 1598-1601, p. 346).

(iii) 1603. Allowance to William Gossone for mourning livery at the funeral of Queen Elizabeth (H. C. De Lafontaine, The King's Musick [n.d.], p. 46. See also W. Nagel, Annalen der englischen Hofmusik [Leipzig, 1894], p. 35).

(iv) 1606-7. His name in list of musicians receiving annuities and fees from the crown (Nagel, p. 37).

(v) Marriages: April [should be May] 14, 1617. William Gosson, of the Parish of St Olive, in the Co of Surrey, gent., and Faith Towell, of the parish of St Giles without Criplegate, widow, late wife to Anthony Towell, of the parish of St Catherin Cree Church, London, vintener, deceased, pr. lic. Nich. Kempe (Register of St. Botolphe's, Bishopsgate, ed. Hallen, I, 56).

(vi) August 18, 1620. William Gosson, drum major, ordered

to impress twenty-eight drummers for service against the Algeria
pirates (State Papers Dom.,1619-23, p. 172).

(vii) May 12, 1625. Referred to as drum major in list of
King James's servants (Historical MSS Commission: Twelfth Report
Coke MSS, XL, 195; see also de Lafontaine, p. 57).

(viii) July 15, 1628. His name in list of musicians dis-
charged from paying the five subsidies lately granted by Parliament (De Lafontaine, p. 67).

(ix) April 20, 1629. Will of "William Gosson of the Cittie of Westminster in the Countie of Middlesex Esquire, Drumme
Major to the kings most excellent majestie being at this present
sick in bodie but of godd and perfect memorie." Directs that
he be buried "in the parrish church of St. Margarett in Westminster aforesaid as neere unto the pew" where his wife customarily
sits as possible. Leaves 40 shillings to the poor of the parish;
10 shillings to "Vincent Peirs Doctor of Divinitie"; 10 shilling
to "Mr. John Harris Lectorer of the said parrish" to preach his
funeral sermon; to "my Cosen Dorothy Goodwin widdow dwellinge
at New Castle [apparently Stephen's "my welbeloved neece Dorothy
Mansworth"], my gold ringe sett with a stone called a Cattseye,"
and the furnishings of "my forechamber where I now ly," and,
after the death of his wife, "my three houses or tenementes...
in the Cloth faier in the parrishe [of] greate St. Bartholo-
mewes...which I hold by lease under the right Honorable the
Earle of Holland"; to "my Cousin Margaret Chamflower [appar-
ently Stephen's "my Cozen Margaret Oxenbridge"] my Spannish
bedsteed the iron pott which was my late brothers, and my black
leather chaire which was my said late Brothers"; 20 shillings
to "my maid servant Elizabeth Lockhead"; the residue of his
estate to his "welbeloved wife ffaith Gosson," whom he makes
sole executrix of his will. "And I doe desier my sonne in
lawe Anthony Jeffes to be overseer of this my last will, and
to be aidinge and assisting as much as in him lieth to my
executrix his mother." Proved at London, May 5, 1629, by Faith
Gosson, executrix. (36 Ridley, Prerogative Court, Canterbury).

(x) Burials: April 22, 1629. Mr. William Gosson
(Memorials of St. Margarets Westminster).

(xi) May 5, 1629. Robert Tedder sworn drum major in the
place of "William Goshen, deceased" (De Lafontaine, p. 69).

APPENDIX B

BIBLIOGRAPHY

I. Genuine Works

(i) Speculum humanum. Made by Stephen Gosson. A poem of
six eleven-line stanzas printed on the last two pages of H.
Kirton's translation of Pope Innocent III's De Contemptu Mundi:
(1) "The Mirror of Mans lyfe...Englished by H. Kirton. Imprinted at London, by Henry Bynneman. 1576." Not entered in the
Stationers' Register. The Short Title Catalogue (14093) erroneously lists this as the second edition. The only copy known
was in the Harmsworth collection. Gosson's poem was reprinted
in the following works: (2) "The Mirror of Mans lyfe...
Englished by H. K. Imprinted at London, by Henry Bynneman.
1576." The S.T.C. (14092) erroneously lists this as the first
edition; but in the only copy known (British Museum, 4403.d.11)
the sixth line of stanza five in Gosson's poem is omitted,
which shows that the type must have been set up from an earlier
edition. (3) "The Mirror of Mans lyfe...London, by Henry
Bynneman. 1577." S.T.C. 14094. The only copy known is in the
Bodleian, Tanner 838. (4) "The Mirror of Mans lyfe...London,
by R. Robinson. 1586." The only copy known was in the Harmsworth collection. (5) J. P. Collier, The Poetical Decameron
(Edinburgh, 1820), II, 216-18. (6) Select Poetry Chiefly
Devotional of the Reign of Queen Elizabeth, ed. Edward Farr
(Cambridge, 1845), pp. 344-6. (7) The Schoole of Abuse, ed.
Edward Arber (London, 1868), pp. 76-7. Arber printed the poem
from no. 2, which omits the sixth line of stanza five. Arber's
edition was reissued (8) London, 1869; (9) Westminster, 1895.

(ii-iii) Stephan Gosson in prayse of the Translator and
In Thomae Nicholai occidentalem Indiam St. Gosson. The first
a poem of six six-line stanzas, the second twelve lines of
Latin elegiacs, commendatory verses prefacing Thomas Nicholas's
translation of Lopez de Gomara's La Conquista de Mexico:
(1) "The Pleasant Historie of the Conquest of the VVeast India,
...Translated out of the Spanishe tongue, by T. N. Anno. 1578.
Imprinted at London by Henry Bynneman," S.T.C. 16807. Entered
in the S.R., and a copy lodged, February 7, 1578. Copies in
the Huntington Library and elsewhere. Gosson's verses were

reprinted in the following works: (2) The Pleasant Historie
(London, 1596). S.T.C. 16808. Copies in the New York Public
Library and elsewhere. (3) The Schoole of Abuse, ed. Edward
Arber (London, 1868), pp. 77-8; reissued (4) London, 1869;
(5) Westminster, 1895. (6) The Pleasant Historie (New York,
1940)--Scholars' Facsimiles and Reprints.

     (iv) Steuen Gosson in prayse of the Booke. A commendatory
poem of two six-line stanzas printed on **4^v of: (1) "Florio
His firste Fruites...Imprinted at the three Cranes in the Vin-
tree, by Thomas Dawson, for Thomas Woodcocke." S.T.C. 11096.
Entered in the S.R. August 23, 1578; epistle at end dated August
10, 1578. Copies in the Bodleian, British Museum, and Huntington Library. Reprint: (2) ed. Arundell del Re (Formosa,
Japan, 1936). The verses were not printed by Arber, who was
unable to find a copy of Firste Fruites.
     It can be assumed with a high degree of certainty that the
above four poems are the only ones that appeared in print over
Gosson's name. Professors V. B. Heltzel and F. B. Williams, Jr.,
who have compiled extensive catalogues of Elizabethan commendatory verses, both searched their files for me and reported that
they could find no other poems by Gosson.

     (v) The Schoole of Abuse, London, 1579. Entered to Thomas
Woodcock in the S.R. July 22, 1579. S.T.C. 12097, which erroneously lists all copies dated 1579 as belonging to the same
edition. The bibliographical evidence shows that there were
two separate editions published in that year (one titled The
Shoole of Abuse and the other titled The Schoole of Abuse), and
that the first edition was a double printing, which means that
more than fifteen hundred copies were run off at one time.
For a discussion of the significance of the size of the edition,
see Chapter II, pp. 26-7. I have been able to learn of the
existence of the following nine copies dated 1579 (the letters
in parentheses indicate the abbreviations chosen to designate
each copy):
    (H) Huntington Library, 61175--lacks *1, *8, F6.
    (C) Cambridge University Library, Syn. 8.57.13--lacks *1,
         *8, F5-F6.
    (B) Bodleian, Malone 475--lacks *1, *8, F5-F6.
    (R) The Rosenbach Company--lacks *1, *8, E6-F6, and D4 is
         a photographic facsimile from another copy.
    (F) Folger Library (not seen).
   (BM) British Museum, 1076.a.6--lacks *1, *8, F5-F6, and F4
         is pasted in, being the corresponding leaf (F7)
         from a copy of the 1587 edition.
   (Bl) Bodleian, Linc. 8° F 200--lacks *1, *8, E6-F6.

(Hn) Huntington Library, 61176—lacks *1-*8, B2, F5-F6.
(E) Emmanuel College, Cambridge (not seen).
(1) Huntington 61175:
[Within a border of type ornaments] The/ Shoole of Abuse,/
Conteining a plesaunt in-/ uectiue against Poets, Pipers,/
Plaiers, Iesters, and such like/ Caterpillers of a Comonwelth;/
Setting vp the Flagge of Defiance to their/ mischieuous exer-
cise, & ouerthrow-/ ing their Bulwarkes, by Prophane/ Writers,
Naturall reason, and/ common experience:/ A discourse as
pleasaunt for/ Gentlemen that fauour lear-/ ning, as profitable
for all that wyll/ follow vertue./ By Stephan Gosson. Stud.
Oxon./ Tuscul. 1/ Nædare literis cogitationes, nec eas dispo-/
nere, nec illustrare, nec delectatione a-/ liqua allicere
Lectorem, hominis est in-/ temperanter abutentis, & otio, &/
literis./ Printed at London, by Thomas/ VVoodcocke. 1579.
      *2-*7, A-E8, F5. Folios A-E5 numbered 1-37. 1-3, 5, 7,
9, 11-16 not numbered; 34 misnumbered 33, 36 misnumbered 35.
[*]   Wanting, was probably blank
[*2] Title page, verso blank
*3   Head title: [Leaf] To the right noble/ Gentlemā, Master
       Philip Sidney/ Esquier, Stephan Gosson wisheth health/
       of body, wealth of minde, rewarde/ of vertue, aduaunce-
       ment of honor, and/ good successe in godly/ affayres.
       Roman and Italic. R-T [*3ᵛ-*6] The Epistle/ Dedicatorie
[*6ᵛ] No head title. Roman and Italic. R-T [*6ᵛ-*7ᵛ] To the
       Reader
[*8]   Wanting, was probably blank
A   Head title: [paragraph sign] The Schoole of/ Abuse. Black
       Letter and Roman. R-T [Aᵛ-E5] The Schoole/ of Abuse.
[E5ᵛ] Blank
[E6]   Head title: To the right Honora-/ ble sir Richard Pipe
       knight, Lord Ma-/ ior of the Cittie of London, & the
       right/ worshipful his brethrē, Continuance of/ health
       and maintenance of Ciuil gouernement. Roman and Italic.
       R-T [E6ᵛ-F] To the Lord Maior/ of London.
[Fᵛ]   Head title: To the Gentlewomen Citi-/ zens of London,
       Flourishing/ dayes with regarde of Credite. Italic
       and Roman. R-T [F2-F4ᵛ] To the Gentlewomen/ of London.
[F5]   Woodcock's device (McKerrow, No. 247), verso blank
[F6]   Wanting, was probably blank
Except for some slight variations, C, B, and R conform to the
above description.
      (2) British Museum 1076.a.6:
[Within a border of type ornaments, left border containing a T
near bottom, right border containing a D near bottom] The/
Schoole of Abuse,/ Conteining a plesaunt in-/ uectiue against
Poets, Pipers,/ Plaiers, Iesters, and such like/ Caterpillers

of a Cōmonwelth;/ Setting vp the Flagge of Defiance to their/ mischieuous exercise, & ouerthrow-/ ing their Bulwarkes, by Prophane/ Writers, Naturall reason, and/ common experience:/ A discourse as pleasaunt for/ Gentlemen that fauour lear-/ ning, as profitable for all that wyll/ follow vertue./ By Stephan Gosson. Stud. Oxon./ Tuscul. l./ Mādare literis cogitationes, nec eas dispo-/ nere nec illustrare, nec delectatione a-/ liqua allicere Lectorem, hominis est in-/ temperanter abutentis, & otio, & literis./ Printed at London, for Thomas/ VVoodcocke. 1579.

No colophon. 8vo. *2-7, A-E8, F4. Folios A-E5 numbered 1-37. 1 not numbered, 19-23 misnumbered 20-24, 33 misnumbered 36.

*   Wanting, probably blank
[*2]   Title page; verso blank
*3   Head title: [Leaf] To the right noble/ Gentlemā, Master
              Philip Sidney/ ... Roman and Italic. R-T The Epistle/
              Dedicatorie.
[*6ᵛ] No head title. Roman and Italic. R-T To the Reader.
A   Head title: [paragraph sign]The Schoole of/ Abuse. Blacl
              Letter and Roman. R-T The Schoole/ of Abuse.
[E5ᵛ] Blank
[E6]   Head title: To the right honorable/ Sir Richard Pipe,
              Knight, Lorde/ Maior of the Citie of London, and the/
              ...R-T To the Lord Mayor/ of London. Roman and Italic.
[Fᵛ]   Head title: To the Gentlewomen Ci-/ tizens of London,
              Flourishing/ dayes with regarde of/ Credite. Italic
              and Roman. R-T To the Gentlewomen/ of London.
[F4]   Wanting; similar leaf from 1587 ed. pasted in

Though all the copies are fairly similar as far as their general description is concerned, when the gatherings of each are compared closely with the corresponding gatherings in the other copies, it becomes evident that the sheets were printed from at least three different settings of type. This can be illustrated by a selected list of catchwords from five copies:

	*3	A3ᵛ	B3ᵛ	Cᵛ	D	E	F4
H	turned	to	liked.	were	tuskes	the	in
C	turned	to	liked,	were	tuskes	the	in
R	turned	to	liked,	were	with	the	(Wanting in)
BM	and	when	he	would	with	his	(R, BM, Bl.)
Bl	and	when	he	would	tuskes	his	(Hn--sicke)

But variations in catchwords provide only partial evidence for the resetting of a forme. More complete collations reveal still further divergences--differences in spelling, reordering of the contents of pages, etc.--that indicate completely new settings

of type. If we designate the setting of type in each gathering
of copy H by the letter x, and gatherings in other copies printed from different settings of type by the letters y and z, we
can show the composition of the various copies by the following
table (minor variations between gatherings, not sufficient to
show a new setting of type, are indicated by apostrophes):

Gathering	H	C	B	R	BM	Bl	Hn
*	x	x	x'	x''	z	z	-
A	x	x	x	x	z	z'	z''
B	x	y	y'	y''	z	z	z
C	x	x	x	x	z	z'	z''
D	x	x	x	y	y	x	y
E	x	x	x	x	z	z	z
F	x	y	y	-	z	-	z

From this table it is clear that H, C, B, and R (and probably F) belong to a single edition, the copies of which were made
up indiscriminately from two different settings of type; and that
BM, Bl, and Hn (and probably E) also belong to a single edition,
the copies of which, except for gathering D, were printed from
still a third setting of type. The fact that the type of gathering D had not yet been distributed when the second edition was
printed shows that the second edition was prepared only a very
short time after the first.

Of the three settings of type, in most gatherings x yields
an inferior text that is poorly punctuated and contains several
typographical errors; in the y setting the spelling and punctua-
tion is improved; but z gives the best text of all. Though z
omits one short phrase ("Quantum mutatus ab illo?" B8^V) and
three marginal notes, it adds six new marginal notes and contains
several revisions that could only have been made by the author
himself. Thus x and y have the phrase "degenerate children" in
C6, z has "vnnatural children;" x and y have "the discourses of
my Phyalo" in F4^V, z has "the Ephserides of Phialo." The fact
that the 1587 edition, which was put out by the same publisher,
was set up from a copy composed of z sheets, also indicates
their superiority over the sheets of x and y. The next time
the Schoole of Abuse is printed, British Museum 1076.a.6 should
be used as the copy text, and variant readings should be given
from Huntington 61175.

(3) Huntington 61177:
The/ Schoole of Abuse,/ Contayning a pleasaunt inue-/ ctiue
against Poets, Pipers, Players, Iesters,/ and such like Caterpillers of a Common wealth;/ ...[13 lines]...Imprinted at London
for/ Thomas Woodcocke. 1587.
    A-F8. Unpaged.
[A]   Title page, verso blank
A2   Head title: [Leaf] To the right noble/ Gentleman, Master

Philip Sidney/ ...Roman and Italic.
[A4ᵛ] No head title. Italic and Roman. R-T To the Reader
[A5ᵛ] Head title: The Schoole of/ Abuse. Black Letter and
        Roman
[E8ᵛ] Blank
F   Head title: To the right honerable/ Sir Richard Pipe,....
        Roman and Italic
[F4ᵛ] Head title: To the Gentlewomen Ci-/ tizens of London,....
        Roman and Italic
[F8] Woodcock's device (McKerrow, No. 247), verso blank
S.T.C. 12098. Other copies: Bodleian, Tanner 67(3)--lacks E8-
F8 (The Princeton University Library copy of the 1579 Ephemeri-
des has bound in at the end eight leaves, the whole of gathering
F, from a 1587 edition of the Schoole of Abuse; possibly they
came originally from this Bodleian copy.); British Museum, c.12.
d.16--lacks A4-A5; Folger (not seen); The Rosenbach Company;
Advocates Library (not seen). Text from copy of type no. 2.
     (4) "A Collection of Scarce and Valuable Tracts...Selected
from Public, as well as Private, Libraries; Particularly that
of the Late Lord Somers...The Second Edition, Revised,...by
Walter Scott, Esq." III (London, 1810), 552-74. Not included
in the first edition of the Somers Tracts. Text from copy of
type no. 2.
     (5) "The School of Abuse...With an Introduction Regarding
the Author and his Works." London, 1841. Vol. II of Shakespear
Society pubs., ed. J. P. Collier. Text from copy of type no. 1.
     (6) "English Reprints...The School of Abuse...and A Short
Apologie of the Schoole of Abuse...Carefully Edited by Edward
Arber." London, 1868. Text from copy of type no. 2. Reissued
(7) London, 1869; (8) Westminster, 1895.

     (vi) The Ephemerides of Phialo and An Apologie of the
Schoole of Abuse, London, 1579. S.T.C. 12093. Ephemerides
entered to Thomas Dawson in the S.R., November 7, 1579. Epistle
to the students of Oxford dated "5. Kalend. Nouemb. [i.e., Oct.
27, 1579."
     (1) Huntington 61172:
(1) [Within a rule, within a border of type ornaments, left
border near bottom containing a T, right border near bottom containing a D] The Ephemerides/ of Phialo, deuided/ into three
Bookes./ The first,/ A method which he ought/ to follow that
desireth to re-/ buke his freend, when he/ seeth him swarue:
with-/ out kindling his cho-/ ler, or hurting/ himselfe./ The
second,/ A Canuazado to Courtiers in/ foure pointes./ The third,
The defence of a Curtezan ouer-/ throwen. And a short Apolo-/
gie of the Schoole of/ Abuse, against Poets,/ Pipers, Players,
&/ their Excusers./ By Step. Gosson, Stud. Oxon/ Imprinted at

London by/ Thomas Dawson./ Anno. 1579.
    *8, A-L8, M4. Folios A-M4 numbered 1-92, several mis-
numbered.
*   Blank
[*2] Title page, verso blank
*3   Head title: To the right noble Gen-/ tleman, Master
      Philipp Syd-/ ney Esquier, Stephan Gosson/ wysheth
      health and/ happinesse. R-T The Epistle/ Dedicatorie.
[*5] Head title: [paragraph sign] Literarum Studiosis in/
      Oxoniensi Academia/ Steph. Gosson Sal. R-T Literarum
      studiosis./ In Oxonien. Academia.
[*7] Head title: To the Reader. R-T To the Reader.
[*8V] Blank
A   Head title: The Ephemerides/ of Phialo. R-T The Ephemeri-
      des/ of Phialo.
[C7V] Head title: The seconde Booke,/ A Canuazado too/ Courtiers.
[G4V] Head title: [paragraph sign] The third booke, the de-/
      fence of the Curtezan, and her/ ouerthrowe.
[K8V] Blank
L   Head title: [paragraph sign] An Apologie of the/ Schoole
      of Abuse, against/ Poets, Pipers, Players, and/ their
      Excusers. R-T An Apologie of the/ Schoole of Abuse.
[M4V] Colophon
(Some slight variations among copies.)
Other copies: Bodleian, Mason A.A.46; British Museum, c.12.d.
14; The Rosenbach Company-lacks *1; Folger (not seen); Princeton
University Library, EX3757.35.332-lacks *1, L-M4 (but has bound
in at end eight leaves, the whole of gathering F, from a 1587
copy of the Schoole of Abuse).
    (2) "The Ephemerides of Phialo...And a short Apologie...
Imprinted at London by Thomas Dawson Anno. 1586." Description
same as 1579 edition. S.T.C., 12094. Copies: British Museum,
8407.a.36; British Museum, c.12.d.15--lacks L-M4; Huntington,
99064; The Rosenbach Company--lacks *1.
    (3) The Schoole of Abuse, ed. Edward Arber (London, 1868);
pp. 62-75, contains a short passage from the dedication of the
Ephemerides (*3-*3V), the opening section (A-A3), and the
Apologie entire (L-M4V). Arber's edition reissued (4) London,
1869; (5) Westminster, 1895.

    (vii) Playes Confuted, London, 1582. S.T.C., 12095. En-
tered to Thomas Gosson on the S.R., March [should be April] 6,
1582.
    (1) Huntington 61174:
[Within a border of type ornaments] Playes/ Confuted in fiue
Actions,/ Prouing that they are not to be suffred in/ a Christian common weale, by the waye/ both the Cauils of Thomas Lodge,

and/ the Play of Playes, written in their de-/ fence, and other
obiections of Players/ frendes, are truely set downe/ and
directlye aunsweared./ By Steph. Gosson, Stud. Oxon./ S. Cyprian
Non diserta, sed fortia./ London/ Imprinted for Thomas Gosson
dwel-/ ling in Pater noster row at the/ signe of the Sunne.
    [Unsigned]5, A-G8. Unpaged.
[1]   Title page, verso blank
[2]   Head title: To the Right Honorable Sir/ Frances Walsing-
      ham Knight,...
A3   Head title: To the Rightworshipful Gentlemen/ and studentes
      of both Vniuersities,/ and the Innes of Court.
B   Head title: The first Action. R-T [Bᵛ-B8] The Confutation
      Of Playes. [B8ᵛ-G8ᵛ] Playes Confuted.
Other copies: Huntington, 61186; The Rosenbach Company; Bodleia
Douce G.63; Bodleian, Malone 476--lacks title page; British
Museum, c.39.a.33; Cambridge University Library (not seen);
Cosin Library (not seen). The paragraph on B4ᵛ begins with the
words: "And William Lodge..." In the Rosenbach and Huntington
61174 copies a printed slip with the name "Thomas" is pasted
over "William." In the Huntington 61186 copy this printed slip
has fallen off, but marks on the page show that it was once
pasted there.
      (2) "The English Drama and Stage...Illustrated by a Series
of Documents...Printed for the Roxburghe Library. M.DCCC.LXIX."
Ed. W. C. Hazlitt. Confuted printed pp. 157-218.

     (viii) The Trumpet of Warre, London, 1598. S.T.C., 12099.
Entered to John Oxenbridge in the S.R., May 22, 1598.
[Within a double rule] The Trumpet/ of VVarre./ A Sermon preach-
ed at/ Paules Crosse the se-/ uenth of Maie/ 1598./ By M. Steph.
Gosson Parson of Great/ Wigborow in Essex./ [Device of Oxen-
bridge, McKerrow No. 289]/ Printed at London by V. S. for I. O.
dwel-/ ling in Paules churchyard at the/ signe of the Parot.
    A4, B-G8. Unpaged.
[A]   Title page, verso blank
A2   Head title: To the most reuerend Fa-/ ther in God,
      Richard Bishop of London,...
[A4ᵛ] Blank
B   Head title: The Trumpet/ of VVarre.
[G8] Blank
Copies: Princeton University Library, EX3747.35.391; British
Museum, 4474.a.11; Bodleian (not seen); Cambridge University
Library, Syn. 8.59.53. A few extracts are printed in "Pleasant
Quippes for Upstart Newfangled Gentlewomen...To which is added,
Pickings and Pleasantries from The Trumpet of Warre...Totham:
Printed at Charles Clark's Private Press. MDCCCXLVII."

II. Lost Works

(i) Plays. None ever published. For references by Gosson
and Lodge to The Comedie of Captaine Mario (1577), Praise at
Parting (1577), Catilins Conspiracies (1578 or 1579), and possibly to other unnamed plays of Gosson's writing, see Chapter II,
pp. 20-2.

(ii) Sermons. Though Gosson preached for almost forty
years, he published only one sermon, The Trumpet of Warre (1598).
For references to other sermons he delivered, but never had
printed, see Chapter III, pp. 45, 47.

III. Doubtful and Spurious Works

(i) Pastorals. In 1598 Francis Meres, comparing the ancient and modern writers of pastoral poetry, said:
>   Amongst us the best in this kind are Sir Philip Sidney,
> master Challener, Spencer Stephen Gosson, Abraham Fraunce
> and Barnefield. (Meres's Treatise "Poetrie," ed. D. C.
> Allen [Urbana, 1933], p. 30)

Later Anthony à Wood, following Meres, wrote of Gosson:
>   He was noted for his admirable penning of pastorals,
> being so excellent therein, that he was ranked with sir Ph.
> Sidney, Th. Chaloner, Edm. Spencer, Abrah. Fraunce, and
> Rich. Bernfield, noted poets of their time. (Athenae
> Oxonienses, ed. Bliss, I, 675)

Since then all Gosson's biographers have attributed to him the
composition of pastorals, though no poetry of that kind has
come down to us under his name.

Meres, as D. C. Allen has shown, is not a trustworthy authority. In preparing his comparisons of English and classical
writers he made "an outline of classical authors first and then
attempted to balance it with an equal number of Englishmen"
(p. 30). Sometimes there were not enough English authors available; so, "for the sake of filling out the numbers of a generic
group," he added names at random. Allen specifies Gosson, Oxford, and Page as among those introduced for the purely mechani-
cal purpose of rounding out a list of names (p. 30). Gosson
did call himself a poet, it is true; but all his statements to
that effect refer specifically, and only, to his composition of
works for the stage. From what we know of his character and
literary interests, we should never suppose that the pastoral
genre would have appealed to him. His genius was adapted rather
to realistic and satiric modes of writing. Furthermore, he was
not the kind of person to hide his light under a bushel, and if
he had written pastorals we may be certain that he would have

mentioned them, as he mentioned his writing of plays.

There is an easy explanation of Meres's error in making Gosson a writer of pastorals. In 1580 appeared A Second and Third Blast of Retrait from Plaies and Theaters. The publication was anonymous, but it was common gossip that Anthony Mundy was the author. In 1583 Mundy published a volume of pastoral poetry, now lost, entitled The Sweet Sobs and Amorous Complaint of Shepherds and Nymphs, which was highly praised by contemporaries. Evidently, Meres confused Gosson, who had written against the stage, with Mundy, who had also written against the stage and had written pastorals.

(ii) Fedele and Fortunio. An English translation of L. Pasqualigo's play Il Fedele (1576), printed in 1585. E. K. Chambers said that, since two lines from the play occur in a thirty-six line poem printed in Englands Parnassus (1600, pp. 417-18) over the initials S. G., "which suggest Gosson," he was inclined "to think Gosson the most likely candidate" for the translator (Elizabethan Stage, IV, 14). If anything is certain about this play, it is that Gosson was not the translator. (1) Only two out of thirty-six lines in the poem are from the play, and they may have been borrowed. (2) The initials S. G. "sugges the names of any number of writers of that period: Samuel Gardiner, Samuel Gilburne, Simion Grahame, etc. (3) A good case has been made out for Anthony Mundy as the translator-- see articles by T. M. Parrott, MP, XIII (1915), 241-51 and M. S. Byrne, The Library, IV (1923), 17-22. (4) When he was connected with the theater, Gosson was ignorant of even the barest rudiments of Italian (see Chapter VI, pp.101), so it would have been impossible for him to translate an Italian play.

(iii) A Short and profitable Treatise, of lawfull and vnlawfull Recreations. J. P. Collier, who had seen only the record entering this work to the publisher Thomas Gosson in the Stationers' Register, suggested that it was a "small tract by Stephen Gosson on his old and favourite theme" (N&Q, 3rd ser., I [1862], 201). Sir Sidney Lee accepted his suggestion and included the work in his bibliography of Gosson's writings in the D.N.B. The treatise was "Written by M. Dudley Fenner, Preacher of the Word of God in Midlebrugh. 1587." Particulars concerning it will be found in the article on Fenner in the D.N.B.

(iv) "A Secret murder hath bene done of late." A sonnet printed in the miscellany entitled The Phoenix Nest (1593). Mr. Hugh Macdonald in his edition (London, 1926, p. 111) notes that "a version of this poem in Rawl. Poet. MS. 85, f. 108^v,

is ascribed to Goss: conceivably a contraction for Stephen
Gosson." H. E. Rollins (The Phoenix Nest [Cambridge, Mass.,
1931], p. xx) dismisses the attribution with the remark that,
though it is "just possible" that the copyist of the MS. intended the abbreviated signature for Gosson, nevertheless, "even
if such an intention could be proved, no evidence exists to
support the ascription." The quality of the poem is low enough
to be within Gosson's capacity; but it is built upon an amorous
Petrarchan conceit such as he never ventured upon in his un-
doubted writings. The poems in the Phoenix Nest appear to be
"to some extent the work of a group of writers more or less
associated," the most important contributors being Dyer, Lodge,
Ralegh, and Watson. Gosson, who engaged in a pamphlet war
with Lodge and criticized the "damned crew," which was associated
in the popular imagination with the atheistical doctrines of
Ralegh and Marlowe, certainly did not belong to this group.
Professor H. H. Hudson (MLN, XLV [1930], 202) has made out a
good case for Ralegh's authorship of the sonnet. I see no
reason for assigning it to Gosson.

(v) To IDEA. A commendatory sonnet, signed S. G., prefacing Michael Drayton's Endimion and Phoebe (1595). Joseph
Ritson suggested that S. G. stood for Stephen Gosson, though
Collier characterized his speculation as "desperate." For once
I agree with Collier. There is nothing to indicate any
association between Gosson and Drayton. The letters S. G.
are not sufficient evidence, because several other writers
of the time had the same initials.

(vi) Pleasant Quippes for Vpstart Newfangled Gentlewomen.
A poem of forty-nine six-line stanzas directed against "The
Fantastical Forreigne Toyes, daylie vsed in Womens Apparell,"
printed at London by Richard Jones in 1595 (S.T.C. 12096), and
again in 1596, with no indication of the author. The first
modern scholar to notice the poem was Sir Egerton Brydges, who
in 1815 referred to it as anonymous and quoted a few stanzas
from it in his Restituta (III, 256-57). In 1841 J. P. Collier,
in the introduction to the Shakespeare Society edition of the
Schoole of Abuse, attributed it to Gosson, saying:
> The authorship of Gosson is ascertained by the
> existence of a presentation copy, of the second
> edition of 1596, with the words Authore Stephen
> Gosson, in his own hand-writing, on the first leaf.
> As it is a great literary curiosity, and as this
> is the first time it has been mentioned as the
> production of so distinguished an author, we may be
> excused for adding some quotations from it. (p. xi)

He thereupon quoted more than half of the poem. As I showed in a communication to the Times Literary Supplement (October 29, 1938, pp. 693-94), the manuscript note on which Collier based has attribution is a forgery, and there is no other evidence to connect the poem with Gosson.

Except for Collier's references, the unique exemplar of the second (1596) edition of the poem was unknown until recently, when Mr. W. S. Wright informed me of its existence in the Dulwich College library. By kind permission of the governors of the college I was allowed to have the pamphlet photographed. It was exactly as Collier had described it, except that the manuscript note read "Auctore Stephen Gosson," and not, as Collier printed it, "Authore Stephen Gosson." The difference in spelling is significant, because the usual sixteenth-century form is "authore." Evidently Collier afterwards realize this and corrected the spelling when he came to print, though obviously he could not rectify the manuscript note he had originally written. Furthermore, when writing a Christian name in Latin it was the custom in the sixteenth century, and the practice of Gosson (see Ephemerides, *6^V), to give it an inflectional ending. Thus we should expect "Authore Stephano Gosson," or better, "Ab Authore Stephano Gosson."

Captain R. B. Haselden compared the note in the pamphlet with examples of genuine Gosson autographs I provided him, and also came to the conclusion that the note was a forgery. He pointed out that, though the general form of the letters in the note is similar to Gosson's ordinary handwriting, the final n's in "Stephen" and "Gosson," instead of ending with a light tapering stroke as do those in genuine autographs, end with a blunt and partly smudged stroke, indicating that they had been carefully traced. Also, the G in the last name begins with a ligature which Gosson only used when he abbreviated his name "Steph: Gosson" and was able to carry over his stroke from the top of the h. Apparently Collier was clumsy both in his penmanship and in his spelling.

The location of the book at Dulwich is in itself cause for suspicion, for it shows that Collier had ample opportunity, and for him ample temptation, to commit the forgery. In the preface to his edition of the Schoole of Abuse he said, "We were led, in the first instance, to Gosson's tract [the Schoole of Abuse], by his connection with Edward Alleyn, late in life, when Gosson was vicar of the parish in which that great actor and most benevolent man was born" (p. v). Earlier in the same year Collier had published the Memoirs of Edward Alleyn, in which he printed two letters by Gosson from manuscripts in Dulwich College, so that he was perfectly acquainted with Gosson's handwriting. In 1843 he published the Alleyn Papers, and in

1845 his edition of Henslowe's Diary. All of these works were edited from manuscripts in Dulwich College, and in all of them he interpolated many forgeries.

The poem contains nothing that is beyond Gosson's literary capability; but it is in character different from his authenticated work. Though he was no prude, neither was he a muckymouthed Mercutio, and it is hardly to be expected that, after settling down as a beneficed clergyman, he would go to extremes of vulgarity far beyond the limits he allowed himself in his pamphleteering days. Pleasant Quippes is coarser in expression than anything Gosson ever wrote.

The poem is a bibliographical rarity, there being only two copies extant of the 1595 edition (one in the Huntington Library and one in the Folger Library), and one of the 1596 edition (in the Dulwich College Library). As he did with other of his forgeries, Collier pushed its publication, and the annual report of the Percy Society, May 1, 1841, announced that it would be printed "during the ensuing year." It duly appeared as a sixteen-page pamphlet--"Pleasant Quippes for Newfangled Gentlewomen, etc. The Percy Society, Vol. XXXI. London, 1841"; but the reprint is not ordinarily found in the files of the Percy Society, because it was suppressed before publication. Five other editions of the poem were published in the nineteenth century. Professor E. J. Howard is at present preparing a scholarly reprint, with an introduction containing full bibliographical details of the various editions, which is scheduled for publication by the Anchor Press this year.

(vii) "In Paradise of late a Dame begun." A poem of six six-line stanzas printed over the initials S. G. in Englands Parnassus (1600), pp. 417-18. Charles Crawford in his edition of the miscellany (Oxford, 1913), p. 517, remarked: "It is thought that by 'S. G.' is meant Stephen Gosson, but there is nothing except identity of initials to favour that opinion." Robert Allott, the compiler of Englands Parnassus, was careless and unreliable and made many false attributions. S. G. may be a misprint for S. T., standing for "Shep. Tonie," the pseudonym of Anthony Mundy. Even if the letters S. G. are correct, there is still no good reason for attributing the lines to Gosson, because there were several sixteenth-century writers with the same initials.